# Can Piaget Cook?

## Mary Anne Christenberry, Ph.D.
## Barbara C. Stevens, Ed.D.

*Contributing author: Jane Caballero, Ph.D.*

Humanics Limited * Atlanta, Georgia

**HUMANICS LIMITED**
P.O. Box 7447
Atlanta, Georgia 30309

Library of Congress Card Catalog Number:  83 – 083224

PRINTED IN THE UNITED STATES OF AMERICA

ISBN: 0 - 89334 - 078 - 2

Illustrations by Mauro Magellan
Cover design by Ann Houston
Typography by Daniel R. Bogdan

*To*
*David Bell and Gunter A. Hameling*

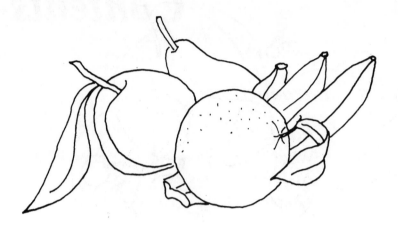

*W*e would like to extend our thanks to the following persons for their assistance in the completion of this book:

Anne Hudson Saunders and the other graduate students in Dr. Christenberry's August College summer practicum.

# Contents

# *Introduction*

*Y*oung children cooking? Of course. . . it is one of the most exciting ways they learn, because it involves *all five senses*. Through food experiences, children learn about measuring, chemical changes, how ingredients combine to make something different, how to read a recipe through both pictures and words, how to plan toward a common goal by sharing responsibilities and working with others. They can see a project, meaningful to them because they will eventually eat the result, carried from the planning stage through production to the final product. They may gain an appreciation of the work involved in producing the food they eat. They see food in various stages of preparation, as they develop small muscle skills (slicing, scraping, cutting, dicing) and large muscle skills through planting and cultivating food.

Not all experiences with food need to involve cooking. Children can slice bananas, apples, and oranges; cut potatoes for block prints; use pudding, catsup, and mustard for fingerpainting; decorate cookies; make

playdough for the housekeeping center; make paste for creative activities; mix paint and starch for art activities; or mix "cookie" dough for baked clay. Although these are common classroom activities, many valuable educational opportunities related to these activities have frequently been overlooked. These opportunities are countless, limited only by the imagination of the teacher. . . and the child.

This book presents a number of suggested learning opportunities using food. Each experience will have stated objectives and suggested extended activities that could be useful to the classroom teacher.

# Chapter 1

## What Piaget Says About Young Children And Ways They Learn

*W*hen Piaget's idea about how children grow, develop, and achieve knowledge first became a topic of general teacher conversation in America in the 1960s, many teachers were at last able to formalize vague insights about gaps between what had commonly been assumed and taught about children's learning and ways they observed them actually working, seeking knowledge, and demonstrating their understanding and thinking in the classroom. David Elkind said it so well: "After a teacher has been introduced to Piaget, she will never again see young children in quite the same way." (Elkind, 1972.)

According to Piaget, intellectual development can be divided into four broad periods or stages. He does not suggest that children move from one discrete stage to another in development, but that cognitive development flows along. The stages he has specified are useful to those of us observing and working with children in conceptualizing the developmental process. However, the development itself has continuity over its entire course.

# Stages or Periods of Intellectual Development as Described by Piaget

### Sensorimotor Period:
*Birth to 2 years*

During this period the child learns through the senses and through manipulation. The child develops awareness that objects remain the same when viewed from different angles.

### Preoperational Period:
*2 to 4 years.*

The child classifies things by a single feature (such as size), with no concern about apparent contradictions (for example, the relationship between size and weight, such as when a large object floats and a small, heavy object sinks). The characteristic phrase for this period is irreversibility.

### Intuitive Period:   *4 to 7 years*

Typical of the child at this age is intuitive (not really understood) classification. The child gradually develops awareness of mass, weight, and volume (for example, the child learns that the amount remains the same even if the substance is transferred to a container of a different size or shape).

### Concrete Operations:   *7 to 11 years*

The child develops the ability to think out problems that previously were "worked" out with concrete objects. The child learns to think logically and to do genuine classification, to organize objects into a series, to reverse operations (as in arithmetic). Abstract thinking does not occur.

### Formal Operations:
#### 11 to 15 years

The child can comprehend abstract concepts. For example, he or she can form "ideals" and reason about the future. The child develops the ability to handle contrary-to-fact propositions and test hypotheses. The child at this age can consider all aspects of a problems and investigate possible solutions.

Piaget affirms that development flows in a cumulative manner (Beihler, 1971) with each new step in development becoming integrated with previous steps. Also, the stages are not independent stages in actual development nor is the chronological age during which children may be expected to develop behavior representative of a particular stage fixed. The age spans suggested by Piaget are *normative* and merely suggestive of the times during which most children can be expected to display the intellectual behaviors characteristic of the particular stage.

Piaget indicates that stages are not automatic (Piaget, 1952). He maintains that the order of the developmental stages is fixed, and the child moves progressively through the four major stages. From birth through adulthood the structures of intelligence (schemata) are constantly developing as the child acts on the environment and assimilates and accommodates to an increasing array of stimuli in his environment. Piaget suggests that four broad factors are related to all cognitive development: 1) maturation, 2) physical experience, 3) social interaction, and 4) a general progression of equilibrium (Piaget, 1961). Movement within and between stages of development is a function of these factors and their actions and none, by themselves, is sufficient to ensure cognitive development.

Piaget's theory is based on the view that older children do not simply know more than younger children, but that the quality or nature of their thought processes are different. Thinking is dominated by what is perceived. The shift from preoperational to logical thought is a gradual process that begins at about five or six and continues until about age nine, when according to Jackson, "the transition from preoperation to operational thinking can be described in terms of the mastery of three types of logical problems: classification, seriation, and conservation." (Jackson, et. al., 1977.)

This transition of growth appears to be primarily a developmental process, and although good teaching methods may enhance the child's experience, teachers need to be aware that it may not be possible to rush or change this development, because "logical thinking is not something that can be taught at just anytime, if it can be taught at all." (Copeland, 1974.)

A major role for teachers of young children is to provide experiences that enable the child to develop concepts through the situations that are provided in the environment. It is well-established through the work of Piaget and others that concepts have their origins in sensory experiences. This leads to the conclusion that the more varied, involving, and direct those experiences are, the better they develop concepts and expand the child's horizon. Lucy Sprague Mitchell, an early childhood educator, demonstrated years ago that when children have opportunities to actually experience their world and act on their immediate environment, they develop complex understandings of that world. Mitchell (1934) said:

"At five, I believe they seldom reach further than the range of their own firsthand explorations. The things that he is told about, but which do not start specific associations of muscles, eye or ear or of some sensory apparatus, are not genuinely intelligible to a five year old."

Food experiences, therefore, are most appropriate. Food is a familiar object that children know, enjoy, and can experience through all five senses. Food experiences may be used in all phases of the curriculum since, for the young child, according to Seefeldt (1977), "there is no separation of disciplines, for children's learning is all of a piece. All teaching and all learning in preschool and primary classrooms are integrated. . . . There can be no artificial separation between subjects with young children."

Learning aids such as films, television, illustrations, and other materials commonly used in the classroom are not nearly as meaningful as the real thing, according to Piaget. He believes that they may produce "figurative" processes rather than operational or logical processes, and that:

> ". . . what we 'see' produces a mental copy or impression of what is seen, but that may be all that it is, a copy. . . in contrast to producing a flexible, reversible, stable understanding of the principles involved."
> — Piaget, 1970

This true understanding presumably may be achieved by using the real thing (for example, food experiences).

Seefeldt maintains:

> "An abundance of natural materials, with the freedom and time to use them, sets the stage for using all of the thinking skills. . . nothing can compare to real objects, to things that children can see, hear, touch, smell, or even taste for themselves. Real objects help children to understand. . . any object that would foster knowledge is appropriate."

Food in the primary and preschool classroom? Of course! It is one of the most powerful teaching tools.

### *Implications for Education*

A brief summary of the educational implications of Piagetian Theory as viewed by various authors is included for persons interested in pursuing this area of educational research.

For many years, Piaget has studied the process of developing intelligence. As translations in America were made in the early 1960s, Piagetian concepts found their way into the writings of Ausebel, Brunner, and Hunt; and Americans soon focused on cognitive development. Burgess identified implications for early childhood education that she felt were clear in the theories of Piaget and of American investigators who were strongly influenced by Piaget: a) Sensorimotor experience is vitally important: b) Language, especially that which relates to labeling, categorizing, and expressing, greatly influences facility in thinking; c) New experiences are more readily assimilated when built on known experiences; d) Repeated experiences with a thing or an idea in different contexts contribute to the clarity and flexibility of a growing concept of the thing or idea; and e) Accelerated learning of abstract concepts without sufficient direct experiences which are related to the concepts may result in symbols without meaning (Butler, 1970).

Piaget believes that sound pedagogy at any level must begin with a thorough understanding of the child. A consideration of the thought and language of young children is requisite to any program of early childhood education. The young child's inability to internalize rules has considerable educational significance, because formal education involves rules. An implication of Piaget's research on thinking is that formal instruction be delayed until about the age of six or seven when most children can learn rules. The preschool program should start from these fundamental facts: a) Preschoolers do not think or act according to rules; b) Their language is not coordinated with their thinking; c) They believe they know or can recall everything. Piaget suggests that formal instruction is inappropriate and materials should be concrete and action-oriented in the preschool. Preparation for formal education is given by providing children with materials that encourage classification, quantifying, and discrimination and which help them learn the alphabet and numbers. (Elkind, 1971).

Curriculum sequences should be designed with the child's changing cognitive status in mind. If curricula do not take into account children's levels of conceptual development, learning is going to be inefficient.

Readiness to learn is of particular concern to education of primary school children. According to Piaget, a child is ready to develop a particular concept when he has acquired the schemata that are the necessary prerequisites. Children can be expected to differ in their histories of maturation, experience, social interaction, and equilibration, and they can differ in how these factors govern cognitive development. The implication is that wide individual differences in conceptual development can be expected in children. Piaget feels learning takes place in a manner that is orderly, sequential, integrative, and hierarchical. Piaget has been concerned with how concepts develop — not how to develop concepts. His technique has been one of systematic observation, description, and analysis of children's behavior. ("The Cognitive Curriculum," 1972)

Piaget is known for his direct interaction and interview procedure with children. Elkind suggests three aspects of Piaget's interview procedure that seem to have implications for teaching. First, Piaget's use of the child's own questions as a starting point for discussion suggests that the child's intellectual level and spontaneous interests be considered in setting up a personalized curriculum design. Second, Piaget's emphasis on the child's ideas as different, rather than right or wrong, suggests that this approach might be given more emphasis in teaching. Third, helping children check their ideas by posing alternative ones should receive as much emphasis as getting children to discover new ideas. (Elkind, 1972.)

Manipulation of materials is crucial. In order to think, young children need to have objects in front of them that are easy to handle. Teachers should select materials that make the child become conscious of a problem and allow him to look for the solution himself. If he generalizes too broadly, then the teacher should provide additional materials in which counter-examples will help the child to see where he must refine his solution. He should learn from the materials. Raising questions is just as important as knowing how to solve them. The teacher can facilitate a child's tendency to ask questions by having a multitude of materials available that raise questions in the child's mind without giving answers. It is important for teachers to know why various operations are difficult for children and to understand that these difficulties must be overcome if a child is to pass from one level to the next. It is not the stages that are important, but what happens in the transition. Teachers must understand that each stage is the fulfillment of something done in the preceding one and the beginning of something that will lead to the next. It is possible for a child to develop more slowly than another and yet go further in the long run because he spends more time exploring all the possibilities at each new level. It seems probable that assimilation done too quickly may not result in a structure that can be generalized as readily to apply to other situations. (Duckworth, 1973)

Piaget has summarized his philosophy best:

"The principle goal of education is to create men who are capable of doing new things, not simply of repeating what other generations have done — men who are creative, inventive, and discoverers. The second goal of education is to form minds which can be critical, can verify, and not accept everything they are offered. The great danger today is of slogans, collective opinions, ready-made trends of thought. We have to be able to resist individually, to criticize, to distinguish between what is proven and what is not. So we need pupils who are active, who learn early to find out by themselves, partly by their own spontaneous activity and partly through materials we set up for them, who learn early to tell what is verifiable and what is simply the first idea to come to them." (Piaget, 1954)

Piaget, *The Construction of Reality in the Child*

# References

Almy, Millie, Edward Chittenden and Paula Miller. *Young Children's Thinking: Studies of Some Aspects of Piaget's Theory.* New York: Teacher's College Press, 1966.

Beihler, Robert F. *Psychology Applied to Teaching.* Boston: Houghton, Mifflin, Co., Inc. 1971.

Butler, Annie L. *Current Research in Early Childhood Education: A Compilation and Analysis for Program Planners.* American Association for Elementary-Kindergarten-Nursery Educators, 1970.

Caballero, Jane A. *A Comparison of Piagetian Conservation Concepts with Reading Achievement.* Ph.D. Dissertation, College of Education, University of South Carolina, 1975.

Chittenden, E.A. "Piaget and Elementary Science," *Science and Children,* VIIII (December, 1970), 9-13.

Copeland, R.W. *How Children Learn Mathematics: Teaching Implications of Piaget's Research.* New York: Macmillan Publishing Co., Inc., 1974.

Duckworth, Eleanor. "Piaget Takes a Teacher's Look," *Learning Magazine,* II (October, 1973), p. 22-27.

Elkind, David. "Early Childhood Education: A Piagetian Perspective," *Education Digest,* XXXVII (December 1971), p. 28-31.

Elkind, David. "The Development of Quantitative Thinking: A Systematic Replacement of Piaget's Studies," *Journal of Genetic Psychology,* XCVIII (1961), p. 37-46.

Elkind, David. "What Does Piaget Say to the Teacher?" *Today's Education,* LXI (1972), p. 46-48.

Kammi, Constance. "The Piagetian Based Curriculum" tape, Columbia, South Carolina: State Department of Education, n.d.

Mitchell. S. *Young Geographers.* New York: Bank Street College of Education, 1934.

Nuttin, Joseph, Paul Fraisse, and Richard Meili. *Motivation, Emotion, and Personality.* New York: Basic Book, Inc., 1963.

Piaget, Jean. *Judgement and Reasoning in the Child.* London: Routledge and Kegan-Paul, Ltd., 1947.

Piaget, Jean. *Origins of Intelligence in Children.* New York: International Universities Prss, 1952.

Piaget, Jean. *Science of Education and the Psychology of the Child.* New York: Orion Press, 1970.

Piaget, Jean. *The Child's Conception of the World.* London: Routledge and Kegan-Paul, Ltd., 1929.

Piaget, Jean. *The Construction of Reality in the Child.* New York: Basic Books, Inc., 1954.

Piaget, Jean. *The Psychology of Intelligence.* London: Routledge and Kegan-Paul, Ltd., 1947.

Seefeldt, C. *Social Studies for the Preschool Primary Child.* Columbus, Ohio: Charles Merrill Publishing Co., 1977.

Seigler, Robert S. "Formal Operations Reasoning," *The Genetic Epistemologist,* Vol. VI, No. 5, October, 1977.

"The Cognitive Curriculum." tape, Berekely, California: The Far West Laboratory for Educational Research and Development, 1972.

Wadsworth, Barry J. *Piaget's Theory of Cognitive Development.* New York: David McKay Co., 1971.

# Chapter 2

## Children Learn About the Environment:

### Organizing Learning Through Three Basic Concepts Developed Through Food Experiences

*A*ccording to Piaget, the child creates individual reality through accommodating and assimilating new experiences into former experiences. If these experiences occur with real, familiar materials, they are particularly meaningful and may be considered to enhance the cognitive development of the young child. Food, very familiar to the child, may be used as a learning aid in the classroom to develop the three general concepts presented in this chapter.

These concepts are described so that the teacher may use them as a guide in considering the worth and relevance of a particular lesson and the materials involved in it. The specifics of the concepts may or may not be used directly with the children (some of the concepts seem to occur naturally during the normal developmental process), but may provide the teacher with some guidelines concerning appropriate objectives as she plans for her students. The concepts are:

I. ALL FOOD IN OUR ENVIRONMENT HAS BEEN A LIVING THING OR IS THE PRODUCT OF A LIVING THING.

II. THE HUMAN BEING RELATES TO HIS ENVIRONMENT THROUGH HIS FIVE SENSES.

III. ENERGY IS NECESSARY FOR LIFE AND FOR ALL LIVING THINGS TO INTERACT WITH THEIR ENVIRONMENT.

## ALL FOOD IN OUR ENVIRONMENT HAS BEEN A LIVING THING OR IS THE PRODUCT OF A LIVING THING.

A. Living things need to take into themselves specific items from the environment.
1. Air, water, and nutrients are necessary for all living things to live and grow.
   a. All plants need air, water, and nutrients.
      (1) Plants take in air through their leaves.
      (2) Plants take in water through their roots.
      (3) Plants take in nutrients through their roots.
      (4) Green plants make their own food from air, water, and nutrients.
   b. All animals need air, water, and nutrients.
      (1) Animals take in air through their lungs, gills, or skins.
      (2) Animals take in water through their mouth, gills, or skins.
      (3) Animals take in food through their mouths.
   c. Human beings need air, water, and food.
      (1) Human beings are animals.
      (2) Human beings take in air through their lungs.
      (3) Human beings take in water through their mouths.
      (4) Human beings take in food through their mouths.

B. All living things interact with their environment in many different ways.
1. Plants take in air, water, and food in several ways.
2. Animals take in air, water, and food in several ways.
3. Human beings take in air, water, and food in a variety of ways.
   a. Human beings take in air by breathing.
   b. Human beings take in water by drinking.
   c. Human beings take in food by eating.

## THE HUMAN BEING RELATES TO HIS ENVIRONMENT THROUGH HIS FIVE SENSES.

Human beings have five senses to help them identify and understand their environment.

A. Human beings have two ears with which to hear sounds in their environment.
B. Human beings have two eyes with which to see light and objects in their environment.

C. Human beings have a body with which to feel objects in their environment.

D. Human beings have a tongue and a nose with which to taste foods in their environment.

E. Human beings have noses with which to smell odors in their environment.

(See pages 22 – 27 for activities to enhance sensory awareness.)

## ENERGY IS NECESSARY FOR LIFE AND FOR ALL LIVING THINGS TO INTERACT WITH THEIR ENVIRONMENT.

A. Heat is energy.
   1. Heat causes materials to change in form.
   2. Heat causes materials to change in odor.
   3. Heat causes materials to change in taste.
   4. Heat causes materials to change in texture.
   5. Heat causes materials to change in sound.

B. Movement uses energy.
   1. All living things have movement (move by themselves).
   2. Non-living things do not move by themselves.
   3. Movement of living things uses energy.
      a. Plants move.
      b. Animals move.
      c. Human beings move.
   4. Movement causes materials to combine in many ways.
      a. Movement may cause chemical changes.
         (1) Chemical changes may cause changes in form.
         (2) Chemical changes may cause changes in odor.
         (3) Chemical changes may cause changes in taste.
         (4) Chemical changes may cause changes in texture.
         (5) Chemical changes may cause changes in sound.
      b. Movement may cause physical changes.
         (1) Combination of some materials results in a mixture in which all materials in that mixture keep their individual identity.
            (a) Some mixtures do not cause change in form.
            (b) Some mixtures do not cause change in odor.
            (c) Some mixtures do not cause change in taste.
            (d) Some mixtures do not cause change in texture.
            (e) Some mixtures do not cause change in sound.
         (2) Combination of some materials results in a mixture of materials in which chemical and physical changes both occur.

The following activities provide the teacher with some narrative to use in the classroom followed by activities the teacher could use to enhance sensory awareness. The teacher can begin this section by explaining that we have five senses: seeing, hearing, smelling, tasting and feeling, which help us learn about the world. The more we use our senses, the more "aware" we become.

### Sight

The eye is our most important organ for finding out about the world around us. We use our eyes to know things around us, to enjoy and take an interest in the beauty of nature, and to appreciate literature and painting. Our eyes help us carry on almost all of the activities of daily life. We see the different properties of objects and learn to compare them. Objects with similar characteristics can be grouped. The grouping of objects helps us to understand them better.

The eyes can overcome great distances. Our eyes are helpers, for without eyes we could not see pictures in books or magazines. In addition, we wouldn't be able to see the beautiful flowers, trees, animals, food that we eat, and people that we would like to be with.

An eye chart is used by a doctor to examine your vision and see whether or not you need glasses. There are two kinds of charts, a Snellen and an E chart. The Snellen chart is used for people who can read the letters and the E chart is for people who cannot read but can show the direction in which the letter is pointing.

Eyes are like cameras. They take still and moving pictures, with or without color. Eyes set themselves for speed, distance, and brightness of light.

The eye is made up of three layers. The retina, which is the inner layer of the eye is sensitive to light and color. The cornea is in front of the eye's two outer layers. It is clear or open and permits light to enter your eye. The pupil is the opening the the middle layer where it has a black spot. The iris is the thin curtain of tissue which is in the front of the lens.

22

Eyes have eyebrows over them and eyelashes around them. The eyebrows and eyelashes are made of little hairs. They keep dust from falling into the eyes. Eyes have eyelids, too. They are like window shades. They close over your eyes and keep out light so you can go to sleep. They blink to keep out dust.

### Sight Activities:

The following experiences can be used to help make the awareness of sight more meaningful.

1. Recognizing shapes, such as circles, triangles, or squares, in drawings could deepend the awareness of shapes.
2. Color blindness may be detected by playing the color spot test. A picture made up of spots of one color is put on a spotted background of another color. The child is to name the picture.
3. Recognizing small objects or pictures camouflaged in a larger picture will develop the "seeing" of a child.
4. Have a child describe a picture from memory.
5. Have a child put puzzle pieces together to form a picture.
6. Build-a-Letter— Use pipe cleaners or pegs to make the ABC's or numerals.
7. Figure Ground— Find the numbers and color them each with a different color.
8. Bend Light Rays Experiment— Place a pencil in a half a glass of water. Look at it from the top, bottom and sides. Result— when you look at the pencil from the side, the pencil appears to be bent or broken at the point where it enters the water.
9. Look at the objects in the Seeing box under a magnifying glass. Describe what you see.
10. Change the location of five familiar objects in the classroom and have the children find the five changes.

### Hearing

The ear is a delicate organ damaged by infection or injury. If any serious damage comes to the ear, a person can become partly or completely deaf.

Our ears are helpers, too. Our ears help us learn how to talk. Our ears help us to hear and listen to music, our parents, our friends, animal sounds and many things around us. We have high and low, loud and soft sounds.

All sounds are caused by something moving back and forth very fast. It is called vibration. A vibration causes sound waves in the air. When a wind blows leaves, they make a sound. We cannot see sound waves, but we can see what causes them.

We have an eardrum in each ear which starts to vibrate when sound waves hit it. The eardrum causes three little bones to vibrate. The nerves in our ears pick up the vibration and carry the messages to the brain. This is the way we hear.

The parts of the ear are: eardrum, inner, middle and outer ear. Three small bones are found in the eardrum and are called the hammer, anvil and stirrup.

Everyone should take care of their ears. We should never put anything into them, nor pick at them with anything which has a sharp point because it might break the eardrum.

### Hearing Activities:

1. The teacher plays a tape recorder with different sounds with which the children are familiar. Then the children will tell the different sounds they recognize.
2. The child will run his finger down the comb. What does he hear? What happens to the comb's teeth? Do they move?
3. Cut a big window in one side of a milk carton. Stretch a skinny rubber band lengthwise around the carton over the window. Pluck the rubber band. What do you hear? Do the same with a fat rubber band.
4. Tie a metal spoon to the middle of a long piece of string. Hold the ends of the string by your ears. Swing the spoon back and forth. Now swing the spoon so it hits a table. The spoon vibrates so it travels along the string to your ears. Try a bigger spoon and fork. What are the results?
5. Ask the children, "What was the last thing you remember hearing before you went to bed last night?"
6. Each day play a record of nature sounds, such as bird calls, as the children enter the room. Discuss the sounds and see if the children can identify them.
7. Let the students feel sounds by listening to familiar sounds, such as

washing machines, sirens, or dogs barking, on tapes or in musical arrangements. The student can feel the sounds and express them in drawing, painting, or modeling, and have a more meaningful experience than simply identifying a sound by a limited verbal vocabulary.

### Smell

Smell is one of the most important senses in a man or animal. Like sight and hearing, smell gives information about the environment. We can smell objects some distance away, but the nose must come into contact with odor. The sense of smell is more sensitive than that of taste. The olfactory cells are the tiny hairs on the upper part of our nose. Nostrils are the two little openings at the end of the nose. The air goes up your nose and into your head. When it gets into your head, you can smell it. Smells are difficult to organize.

There are three basic types of odors. These are: flowery, such as roses or gardenias; fruity, such as apples, oranges and lemons; and burnt odors such as found in a well-done steak or black toast. Smell helps us to distinguish one food from another. It helps us learn to taste. When a person has a cold, air cannot get through the nose, and so smell or taste is lost.

### Smell Activities:

1. Take a lemon and close your mouth. Hold the lemon in front of your nose. Breathe in through your nose. Can you smell the lemon? Now hold your nose so that you cannot breathe through your nostrils. Hold the lemon in front of your mouth. Breathe in through your mouth. Can you smell the lemon?
2. The teacher blindfolds a child and puts an object under his nose and asks him to determine what it is. For example: food, flowers, soap, perfume, cinnamon, stone, etc.
3. Burn incense in the classroom, varying the scent from day to day.
4. Smell jars: Smelling various familiar liquid solutions, foods or spices, may also give a student a deeper experience in the use of this sense. A solution such as ammonia or smoke (a match or small piece of burning paper), a food such as peanut butter or mayonnaise, and spice such as garlic or cinnamon, could be put in a closed jar. When the lid is removed the child could sniff and see if he can identify the smell.

## Taste

Our tongue is a helper which helps us tell one food from another. The taste buds are bumps on your tongue which are sweet up front, bitter in the back, salty and sour on the sides. The front of the tongue is small and pointed and has fewer taste buds. The back of the tongue has bumps which are larger and rounder.

Food seems tasteless to a person when a bad cold has shut off the passages of the nose. One can't talk very well and doesn't seem to sound right. When you have a cold, air cannot get through your nose. Then you cannot smell or taste. We learn to organize foods and drinks by the way they taste.

## Taste Activities:

1. Apple and onion activity — Blindfold a child. Hold an onion under his nose and put a piece of apple in his mouth. He will think he is eating an onion. Then he can hold his nose while you give him either an apple or an onion. He will have to tell what he ate without using his sense of smell.
2. We have four taste buds. Blindfold a child and ask if the food is sweet, salty, sour or bitter by using and not using the sense of smell.
3. To help develop precise vocabularies, suggest that the children taste and describe contrasting substances such as carrot and celery, marshmallow and corn chips, popcorn and crackers.
4. Without the children's knowledge, sweeten some water with an artificial sweetner (a substance not familiar to them). Have them taste water. Then allow them to watch you to place ordinary water in a glass and add a sweetner to it. Have them taste the water prepared, then ask them to describe any difference between it and the water tasted before. This is a test of the effect of the other sense on the sense of taste.

## Touch

Touch is the sense which gives us notice of contact with an object. We learn the shape and hardness of objects through this sense. Touch gives a person some of the most important knowledge of the objects in the world. When a person touches an object, feelings of warmth, cold, pain or pressure are received.

The feeling of pressure has the biggest number of sense organs. It is highly developed on the tip of the tongue and is poorest on the back of the shoulders. The tips of the fingers and the end of the nose are other sensitive areas. The nerve endings form small discs, just inside the living layer of the skin. These nerve endings are around each of the hairs in your skin and help your sense of touch.

Touch is pain, pressure, smooth, soft and hard. The senses are in your muscles and bones. When you climb a tree, these senses help you decide what to do and how much force to apply. When you drink something hot or cold, you feel the temperature in your mouth and throat. If you swallow something very hot, you will feel pain. If you miss a meal or two, your empty stomach will cause you hunger pains. When the amount of water in your body is low, you will feel thirsty.

We can feel with any part of our bodies. We can find out about objects by feeling similarities. Different parts of our bodies are more sensitive to touch than other parts. We can organize the things we feel by the way they feel.

### Touch Activities:

1. Trace different shapes of objects, numbers or letters. Then color the designs. Cookie cutters may be good to use.
2. Awareness of texture and the vocabulary needed to describe it can be further developed in subsequent lessons by having the children touch wet and dry, sponges, hard stones, soft putty and aluminum foil.
3. To increase awareness of the sense of touch, children may put a hand in a grab-bag of familiar objects and feel to see if the common object can be identified. Some easy objects to use in this experience could be a rubber band, paper clip, eraser, or key.
4. Objects with a distinct texture, such as sandpaper or glass, or a distinct temperature, such as ice or an iron (a toy iron could be used for this demonstration) could be displayed. The child could tell what he thought it felt like, then touch it to see if correct.

# Chapter 3

## Lesson Plans for Using Food Experiences in the Classroom:

### Plans for the Whole Year

*Y*oung children must be encouraged to learn numerous facts and practices that will enable them to make intelligent and appropriate decisions concerning healthful daily living and to continue these practices throughout their lifetime. Children must be taught these skills when they are young so that these health practices will become habits. Young children need to learn good habits of personal hygiene, proper table manners and selecting nutritional foods. Activities that will motivate the child to learn about good nutrition may include:

1. Draw foods from the four basic food groups, color them, and cut them out. Attach strings and hang on a coat hanger to make a food mobile.
2. Have the children keep a record of what they eat daily. Tell them to try to choose from the four basic food groups.
3. Give the children paper plates and have them draw a well-balanced breakfast, lunch and dinner.
4. Allow the children to make simple recipes.

Nutrition awareness is vital if the child is to grow up as a healthy, productive member of society. Good nutrition is essential for normal organ development, growth, optimum activity and working efficiency and for resistance to infection. Since nutrition is the foundation of good health, education is the cornerstone of good nutrition. The individual must be taught how to attain good nutrition, to make good food selections and understand his changing nutritional needs. We, as educators, should achieve the following objectives: 1) Provide food that will help meet the child's total nutritional needs, while recognizing individual and cultural food differences; 2) Involve parents and community agencies in the nutrition program; 3) Use mealtime as a learning experience and provide a clean, pleasant environment; 4) Show the relationship of nutrition to other aspects of life; 5) Help the child and his family understand good nutrition and how to develop healthful food habits.

### *Nutrients: The Essentials of an Adequate Diet*

Certain chemical substances needed by the body are called nutrients. A nutrient is a chemical substance found in food. These nutrients are substances made up of combinations of chemical elements. The nutrients are divided into six groups: 1) Carbohydrates, 2) Proteins, 3) Fats, 4) Vitamins, 5) Minerals, and 6) Water. It is necessary to provide the body with adequate nutrients needed. The amounts needed are dependent on age, sex and activity. Children need more energy than adults because they are growing. A brief summary of these nutrients follows.

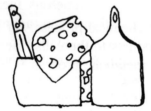  

*Carbohydrates* — starches and sugars in foods that serve as the main source of energy. They contribute about 45 percent of the calories in a well-balanced diet. Starches are found in bread, cereals, flour and potatoes. White or brown sugar are the most common sources of sugar known as sucrose; however, lactose is found in milk.

*Proteins* — necessary for growth and maintenance of body structures. Bones, muscles, skins, and other solid parts of the body are made up largely of proteins. They provide energy and make up about 12 to 15 percent of the diet's calories. Animal proteins are found in cheese, eggs, fish, meats, and milk. Vegetable proteins are found in beans, grains, nuts and vegetables.

*Fats* — a source of energy that furnishes a little more than 40 percent of the calories in the diet. Nurtitionists classify fats as visible or invisible. Visible fats are butter, oil and shortening that are added to food. Invisible fats incude the butterfat in milk and fats in eggs, fish, meats and nuts.

*Vitamins* — essential for good health. Food must supply the body with vitamins. Some vitamins include:

*Vitamin A:* found in green and yellow plants and fish liver and fish oils. It is necessary for healthy skin and development of the bones.

*Vitamin B1 (thiamin):* found in whole grain cereals and meats. It is necessary for the use of starches and sugars in the body.

*Vitamin B12:* found in animal products, such as liver and folic acid: found in leafy green and yellow vegetables. These are needed for the formation of red blood cells and proper functioning of the nerves.

*Vitamin C (ascorbic acid):* found in fruit (oranges and lemons) and in potatoes. It is needed for the maintenance of the ligaments, tendons and other supportive tissue.

*Vitamin D:* present in eggs, fish-liver oil and liver. It is also formed when the skin is exposed to the sun. It is needed for the use of calcium by the body.

*Vitamin K:* manufactured by bacteria in the intestine. It is necessary for the proper clotting of the blood.

*Water:* necessary for every cell, for every chemical process, for the transportation of oxygen and nutritive products to the cells, for the removal of carbon dioxide, and for every metabolic process.


Nutritionists have grouped foods according to nutrient content to simplify the planning of a varied diet. The Basic Four (as we all know) are: 1) Milk Group, 2) Meat Group, 3) Bread and Cereal Group and 4) Fruit and Vegetable Group.

*Minerals* — These are needed for growth and maintenance of body structures. Calcium, magnesium and phosphorus are essential parts of the bones and teeth. Calcium is needed for blood clotting. Iron is an important part of the red coloring matter in blood called hemoglobin. Minerals are needed in the digestive juices and fluids in the body cells. Other minerals include iodine, potassium, sodium and sulfur.


### Malnutrition

Malnutrition means poor nutrition or that the body lacks one or more essential foods. It is caused by a poor intake usually stemming from the family living pattern. Poor emotional tones in the environment may be responsible for a child's attitude toward food and eating. Inadequate financial resources will also effect the food intake. Poor eating habits, including hurried meals, eating snacks between meals, dietary fads, and poor selection of foods, also can be related to malnutrition. Malnutrition may be a continuous condition since birth or it may result anytime thereafter. If a child suffers from malnutrition, he needs medical supervision. The causes should be determined, and the teachers should work closely with parents, school nurse, physician and social worker.

Being underweight can be a serious problem that can affect the health and growth of a child. It should also be analyzed and monitored closely.

Overweight/obesity is one of the greatest health problems in the United States. People enjoy eating, and we have a lot of food available. Other causes include inactivity, emotional disturbances, and abnormal functioning of glands or metabolism. For people, the most satisfactory way to reduce weight is to cut down on food containing concentrated sources of energy (sugars, starches, and fats) and continue eating enough protective foods (lean meats, milk, fruits and vegetables).

## Cooking

Adults often hesitate to involve young children in the preparation of food. Teachers in particular, concerned with the time limitations and the mess involved, often fail to understand children's cooking capability. The importance of cooking or food preparation as a learning experience should not be underestimated. Many negative attitudes toward foods or towards helping others may be alleviated during cooking activities. Children who contribute to the preparation of foods often learn to enjoy new types of foods. Children who help set a table for lunch or a snack may take more pride in their work. Objectives for cooking in the classroom include:

1. Promoting the child's sense of accomplishment.
2. Having fun, thus enhancing his self-concept.
3. Promoting cognitive, social, and cultural learning experiences.
4. Utilizing sensory perceptions.
5. Learning about the colors, shapes, and sizes of foods.
6. Learning about units of weight and measurement.
7. Learning proper use of kitchen tools and utensils.
8. Developing new vocabulary words.
9. Following directions.
10. Sharing a group project.
11. Learning proper nutritional habits.
12. Observing physical and chemical changes.

In cooking, as with any activity, certain safety precautions must be observed. Some of these include:

1. Identifying children with food allergies.
2. Using caution when serving foods which may cause choking such as nuts, celery, and popcorn.
3. Encouraging children to sit down while eating.
4. Limiting the number of children to avoid crowding and to allow each to participate.
5. Using child-size furniture.
6. Using unbreakable equipment, if possible.
7. Having enough utensils for all the children. Use blunt knives for cutting.
8. Supervising cooking carefully or having adults do the actual cooking over the burners.
9. Planning the project carefully and discussing the plans with the children.
10. Fastening long hair and floppy sleeves.
11. Washing hands before beginning.
12. Allowing adequate time for exploring the foods: observing, tasting, discussing.
13. Providing recipe pictures when possible.
14. Beginning with simple recipes that require little cooking.

These lessons are organized according to a sequence of experiences a teacher might undertake in the course of a year in a typical classroom. The recipes range from simple to more involved food experiences for children. This is the only sequence implied by the arrangement of the lesson plans and recipes in this chapter. Indeed, you may begin anywhere in the chapter with any concept you wish and develop your own sequence.

The lesson plans and recipes have all been tested and refined by teachers and children in actual classroom settings. We have sought, considered, and implemented suggestions from both children and their teachers.

Have fun doing these experiences with your own class. Remember to put your own imprint on them. These lessons are intended as only a guide to get your started developing your own ideas and plans.

### Tips as You Start

1. Begin with simple recipes or food-related experiences. Use only a few ingredients. Food which can be prepared rapidly and easily with a minimum of assistance and/or immediate guidance of the teacher.
2. Gather all materials, implements and/or appliances together

before the food experience is to take place.

3. Prepare written or oral (on cassette) directions appropriate to the level and/or abilities of the children so that they may assume responsibility and carry through as independently as possible on an assignment.

4. Ask parents to help supply the appliances, implements and ingredients for the food experiences; parents are also an excellent source for volunteer assistance during the preparation of the food in the classroom.

5. Plan for child evaluation of the experience with a checklist of feelings and reactions to the experience. Use these to alter and improve the experience for later implementation of the ideas.

6. Always relate the food experiences to other phases of the curriculum. While it is a worthy experience by itself, because it involves important interests of the child and first hand experiences with a familiar group of materials (food) and a positive relation to this part of his environment, it is a powerful mode of instruction for learning basic skills and concepts.

The recipes in this chapter may be used in any classroom equipped with an electrical outlet; when cooking is involved, it is all done with portable appliances. Some experiences require the use of a refrigerator and it is recommended that the teacher supply a portable ice chest with frozen coolant (water frozen in milk jugs will work) for preservation of ingredients until time to use them if a refrigerator is not available. It is suggested that a teacher select those food experiences comfortably within the scope of the limitations imposed by her classroom circumstances. (There may be possibilities not immediately obvious such as the refrigerator in the teachers' lounge, donation of a refrigerator by an interested parent for the entire primary wing if several teachers are interested in food experiences in the classroom, temporary loan of a refrigerator by an interested parent, the principle, and the like).

All of the recipes included in this chapter meet the following general guidelines:

1. All food needing cooking may be cooked on/in a portable appliance.

2. The recipes contain no more than five ingredients.

3. The experience must be useful to more than one aspect of the child's learning.

4. Sweet, dessert-like foods have been avoided except where the educational value justified their inclusion (i.e., the chemical changes in baking the "rainbow cake").

5. When possible, the food preparation should include a change in form of the ingredients either through chemical change (combination in cooking or mixing) or change in appearance (cutting and/or combining ingredients).

The food experiences have been integrated with literature experiences when appropriate (as "Stone Soup" and "The Big Turnip").

Cooking or preparing, and eating the results, is a natural, interesting, and involving way for children to learn basic concepts of measurement:

> . . . more than
> . . . less than
> . . . fill it up
> . . . pour part of it in
> . . . cut it in half
> . . . give part of it to Susan
> . . . put it all in the bowl
> . . . mix it together
> . . . put the water in the bowl with the flour
> . . . place one spoonful in the pan.

Cooking is also an excellent way for children to learn about chemical reactions. They can observe the variety of forms that substances in the environment can change to:

> . . . water, ice, steam
> . . . cream, whipped cream, butter, buttermilk
> . . . butter, soft butter, hard butter, melted butter
> . . . sugar, icing, syrup, caramel.

As they cook and prepare food, children can see how ingredients change as they are combined:

> . . . milk into powdered pudding
> . . . chocolate syrup into white milk
> . . . bread into toast
> . . . batter into cake and/or pancakes.

As food is prepared, children can see how treatment such as HEATING or FREEZING change the nature of food items:

> . . . milk mixture into ice cream or sherbet
> . . . raw vegetables into softer, sometimes different-looking forms
> . . . raw meat into different textures and flavors
> . . . cheese from firm to semi-liquid form.

35

Sweet foods have been avoided unless the learning to be achieved was deemed worthy of the risk to teeth and the promotion of bad food habits. Too many snacks and treats for young children are basically empty calories with little if any real food value and involve actual harm to the children because of the great appeal of choosing sweet and/or non-nutritional snack foods at the expense of more healthful foods. Many preschool programs for young children have traditionally supplied snacks of sweet drinks and cookies for morning and afternoon snacks when more healthful tastes could be established by providing more nutritious foods.

It has been our experience that food and cooking activities can be among the most meaningful experiences for the child in the classroom. The teacher should get them involved in every phase of the experience from decisions about what to prepare to gathering the ingredients and, of course, preparing the foods. *Get them involved!* If cooking is prohibited in the classroom because of school policy, or the teacher is hesitant about attempting to do it without other adults' help, there are numerous non-cooking food experiences from which children can benefit and which they enjoy.

Cooking should not be attempted by the teacher alone with the children, but may be done with a volunteer from another classroom, an aide, someone from the school office staff, one of the special teachers, or most likely, a community or parent volunteer. The values to be gained by the child from these experiences make it well worth the time, effort, expense, and preparation.

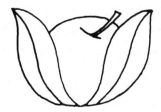

# References

Learning activities utilizing food can be integrated into curriculum areas related to motor skill development, communication and language arts, arithmetic, science, social interaction, music, drama, art and parent involvement.

Numerous educational and commercial sources have developed ideas, materials, cookbooks, games, and other learning activities which the early childhood educator can utilize in making nutrition education the vital, exciting component of the program the topic deserves to be. The following bibliography suggests some of these materials.

Asmussen, P.D. *Simplified Recipes for Day Care Centers.* Cahners Books, 221 Columbus Ave., Boston, Massachusetts 02116, 1973, 217 pp., $12.95.

Association for Childhood Education International. *Cooking and Eating with Children: A Way to Learn.* ACEI, 3615 Wisconsin Ave., NW, Washington, D.C. 20016, 1974, 48 pp., $2.50.

Ault, R. and L. Uraneck. *Kids are Natural Cooks.* Houghton Mifflin Co., One Beacon Street, Boston, Massachusetts 02107, 129 pp., $6.95.

Caldwaller, S. *Cooking Adventures for Kids.* The San Francisco Book Co., Houghton Mifflin Co., 2 Park Street, Boston, Massachusetts 02107, 1974, 101 pp. $6.95.

Cohl, V. *Science Experiments You Can Eat.* J.B. Lippincott Co., Philadelphia, Pennsylvania, 1973.

Cooper, J. *Love at First Bite.* Alfred A. Knopf, New York, 1977, $3.50.

Croft, K.B. *The Good For Me Cookbook.* (Ages 3 – 12), Rand E. Associates, San Francisco, 1971. Order from Karen B. Croft, 741 Maplewood Place, Alto, California 94303.

Ferreira, N.J. *The Mother Child Cookbook: An Introduction to Education.* Pacific Coast Publishers, 4085 Campbell Ave., Menlo Park, California 94025, 1969, 73 pp., $2.85.

Florida Department of Education. *Exploring Foods with Young Children — A Recipe for Nutrition Education.* Food and Nutrition Managment Section, Florida Department of Education, Tallahassee, Florida 32304, 1977, single copy free.

Goodwin, M.T, and G. Pollen, *Creative Food Experiences for Children.* Center for Science in the Public Interest, 1755 S. Street, NW, Washington, D.C. 12009, 1974, 191 pp., $4.50.

Hatfield, A.K. and P.S. Stanton. *Help! My Child Won't Eat Right.*

Acropolis Books, Ltd., 2400 17th Street, NW, Washington D.C. 20009, 1973.

Kargon, M. *Selected Cooking Experiences for Jewish Preschool.* Board of Jewish Education, Early Childhood Department, 5800 Park Heights Ave., Baltimore, Maryland 21215, 26 pp., 1975, $2.50.

Lansky, V. *The Taming of the C. A. N. D. Y. Monster.* Meadowbrook Press, 16648 Meadowbrook Lane, Wayzatta, Minnesota 55391, 1978, $4.45.

Maryland Department of Health. *The Harried Lunch.* Maryland Department of Health, Division of Nutrition, Baltimore, Maryland 1975, single copy free.

McClenahan, P. and I. Jaqua. *Cool Cooking for Kids.* Fearon Publishers, Inc., 6 Davis Drive, Belmont, California 94220, 1976, 170 pp., $6.50.

*Nutrition and Young Children.* Volume 12, No. 1, November, 1978. Children in Contemporary Society, Box 11173, Pittsburg, Pennsylvania 15237, $3.00 (general reference).

Paul, A. *Kids Cooking Without a Stove: A Cookbook for Young Children.* Doubleday and Co., Inc., Garden City, New York, 1975, $5.95.

Pipes, P.L.. *Nutrition in Infancy and Childhood.* The C.V. Mosby Co., 11830 Westline Industrial Drive, St. Louis, Missouri 63141, 1977, $6.95 (general reference).

Ratner, M. and T.T. Cooper. *Many Hands Cooking.* Catalog #5432 UNICEF, 331 E. 38th St., New York, 10016, 1974, $4.00.

Society for Nutrition Education. *Preschool Nutrition Education Monograph,* NNECH Monography No. 3, November 1978, Society for Nutrition Education, 2140 Shattuck Ave., Suite 1110, Berkeley, California 94704, $4.50 (general reference).

Steed, F.R. *A Special Picture Cookbook.* H. & H. Enterprises, Inc., Box 3342, Lawrence, Kansas 66044, 1974.

Veitch, B. *A Child's Cookbook.* 656 Terra California Drive, No. 3, Walnut Creek, California 94595, 1976, 206 pp., $4.50.

Wilms, B., *Crunchy Bananas.* Peregrine Smith, Inc., P.O. Box 11606, Salt Lake City, Utah 84111, 1975, 111 p., $4.95.

Wyden, B. *The Cook Along Book.* David McKay Co., Inc., New York, 1972.

U.S.D.A. *Fun With Good Foods.* Stock No. 001-000-03868-1. Superintendent of Documents, U.S. Government Printing Office, Washington, D.C. 20402, 1978.

USDHEW. *Nutrition Education for Young Children.* U.S. Department of Health, Education and Welfare, Publications No. (ODHDS) 76-31015, U.S. Government Printing Office, Washington D.C. 20402.

# Concept I:
## All Food Has Been a Living Thing
## Or Is the Product of a Living Thing

*Carrot Salad*
*Tops of Plants*
*Fruits in Variation*
*Celery Coloring*
*Beans and Peas*
*Vegetable Prints*
*Group Seed Planting Day*
*Guacamole Dip*
*Cheese and Bean Sprout Sandwich*

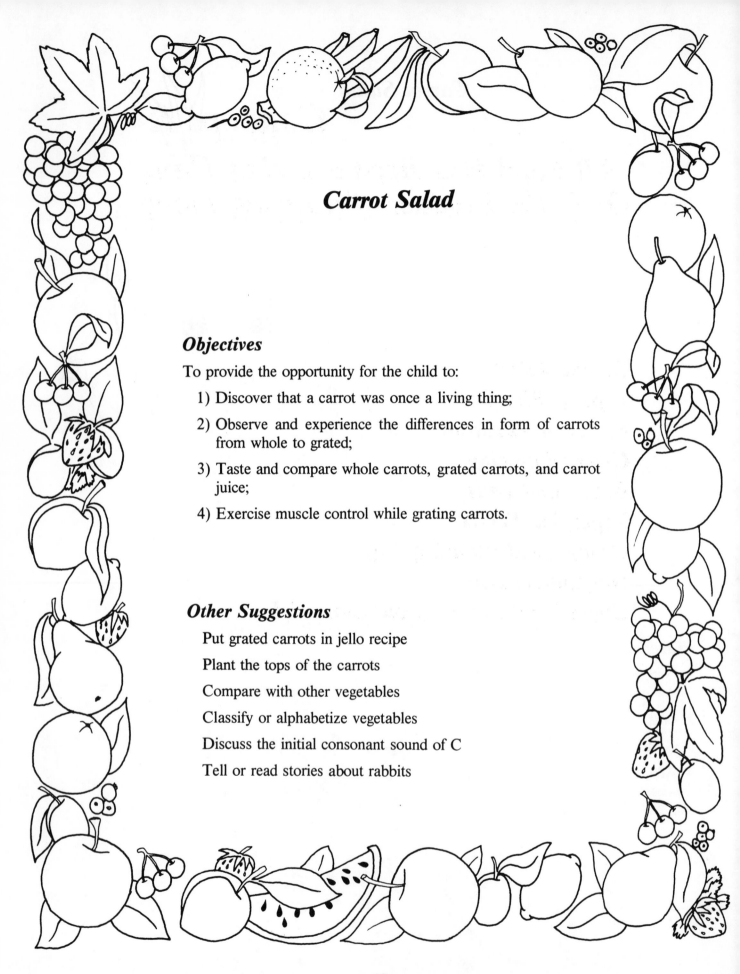

# Carrot Salad

## Objectives

To provide the opportunity for the child to:

1) Discover that a carrot was once a living thing;

2) Observe and experience the differences in form of carrots from whole to grated;

3) Taste and compare whole carrots, grated carrots, and carrot juice;

4) Exercise muscle control while grating carrots.

## Other Suggestions

Put grated carrots in jello recipe

Plant the tops of the carrots

Compare with other vegetables

Classify or alphabetize vegetables

Discuss the initial consonant sound of C

Tell or read stories about rabbits

# Carrot Salad

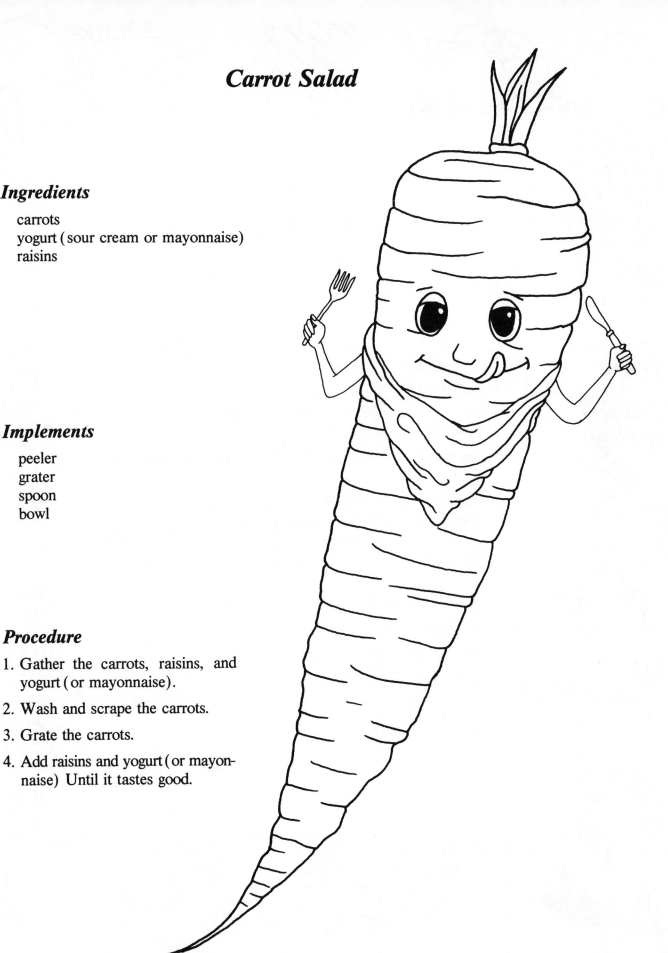

## Ingredients

carrots
yogurt (sour cream or mayonnaise)
raisins

## Implements

peeler
grater
spoon
bowl

## Procedure

1. Gather the carrots, raisins, and yogurt (or mayonnaise).

2. Wash and scrape the carrots.

3. Grate the carrots.

4. Add raisins and yogurt (or mayonnaise) Until it tastes good.

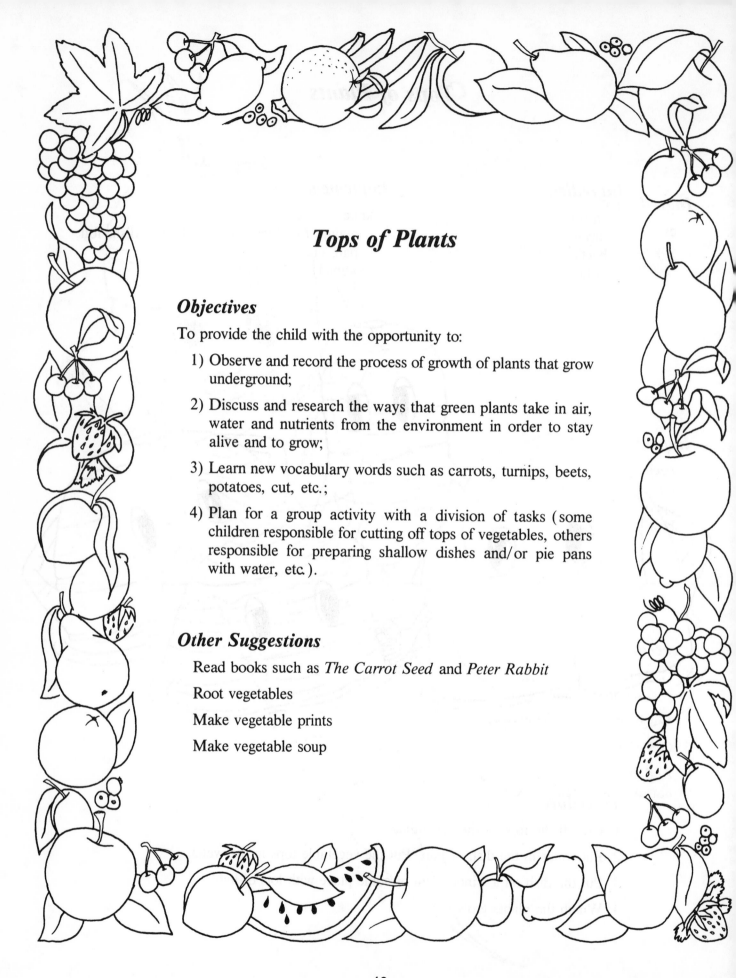

# Tops of Plants

## Objectives

To provide the child with the opportunity to:

1) Observe and record the process of growth of plants that grow underground;

2) Discuss and research the ways that green plants take in air, water and nutrients from the environment in order to stay alive and to grow;

3) Learn new vocabulary words such as carrots, turnips, beets, potatoes, cut, etc.;

4) Plan for a group activity with a division of tasks (some children responsible for cutting off tops of vegetables, others responsible for preparing shallow dishes and/or pie pans with water, etc.).

## Other Suggestions

Read books such as *The Carrot Seed* and *Peter Rabbit*

Root vegetables

Make vegetable prints

Make vegetable soup

# Tops of Plants

## Ingredients

carrots
turnips
beets
potatoes

## Implements

knife
container for water such as shallow dish, foil
    pan, etc.
toothpicks

## Procedure

1. Cut off the tops of the vegetables

2. Put water in the dish or pan. Put the vegetable tops in the water.

3. Put the dish on a window sill or some place with lots of light.

4. Watch the plants grow.

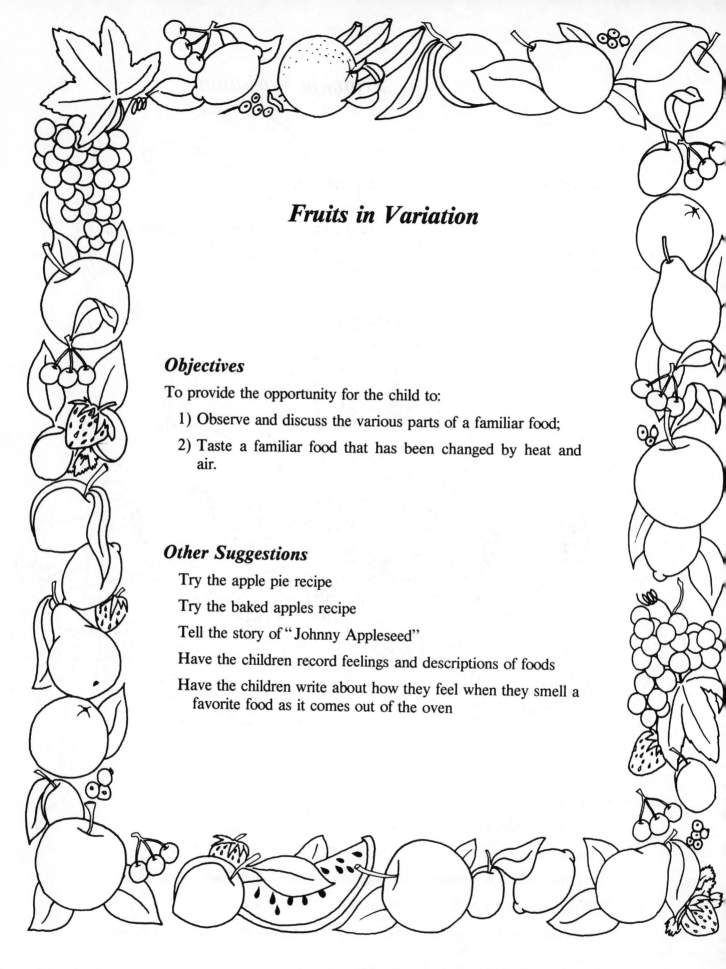

# Fruits in Variation

## Objectives

To provide the opportunity for the child to:

1) Observe and discuss the various parts of a familiar food;

2) Taste a familiar food that has been changed by heat and air.

## Other Suggestions

Try the apple pie recipe

Try the baked apples recipe

Tell the story of "Johnny Appleseed"

Have the children record feelings and descriptions of foods

Have the children write about how they feel when they smell a favorite food as it comes out of the oven

# Fruits in Variation

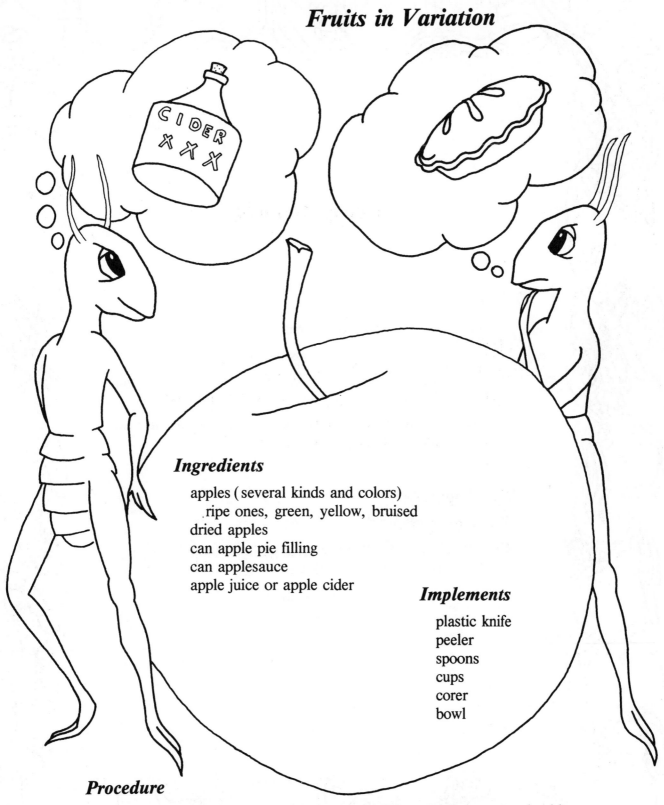

**Ingredients**

apples (several kinds and colors)
 .ripe ones, green, yellow, bruised
dried apples
can apple pie filling
can applesauce
apple juice or apple cider

**Implements**

plastic knife
peeler
spoons
cups
corer
bowl

**Procedure**

1. Gather the apples, dried apples, apple pie filling, applesauce, apple cider.

2. Look at how they are different and alike. Taste them.

3. Set one piece of apple aside and watch the changes as it is exposed to air.

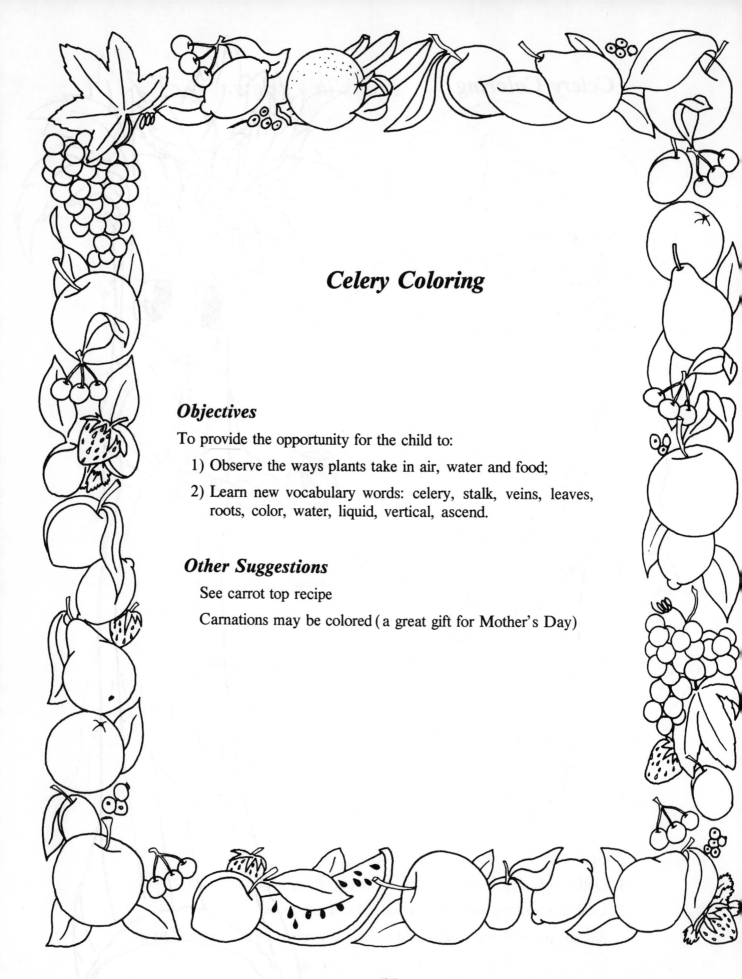

# *Celery Coloring*

## *Objectives*

To provide the opportunity for the child to:

1) Observe the ways plants take in air, water and food;

2) Learn new vocabulary words: celery, stalk, veins, leaves, roots, color, water, liquid, vertical, ascend.

## *Other Suggestions*

See carrot top recipe

Carnations may be colored (a great gift for Mother's Day)

# Celery Coloring

## Ingredients

celery (or carnations)
water
food coloring

## Implements

clear glass or
 plastic jar

## Procedure

1. Gather the celery or carnations and the food coloring.

2. Add one color of food
   coloring to the water.

3. Place the carnation or celery in the colored water
   and set it aside.

4. Observe it the next day —
   what happened?

# Beans and Peas

## Objectives

To provide the opportunity for the child to:

1. Observe vegetables in their pods;

2. Observe inside the pod and the inside of the bean or pea in the pod;

3. Observe growth of a bean that came out of a pod.

## Other Suggestions

Compare peas and beans through the five senses

Cook and compare raw with cooked beans and peas

Make butterflies or collages with pods

Read *Jack and the Beanstalk*

Read nursery rhymes, i.e. "Peas Porridge Hot"

Make chart labeling open seed parts — use as new vocabulary

# Beans and Peas

## Implements

bowl
knife
clear glass jar
paper towel or napkin

## Ingredients

peas in the pod
beans in the pod

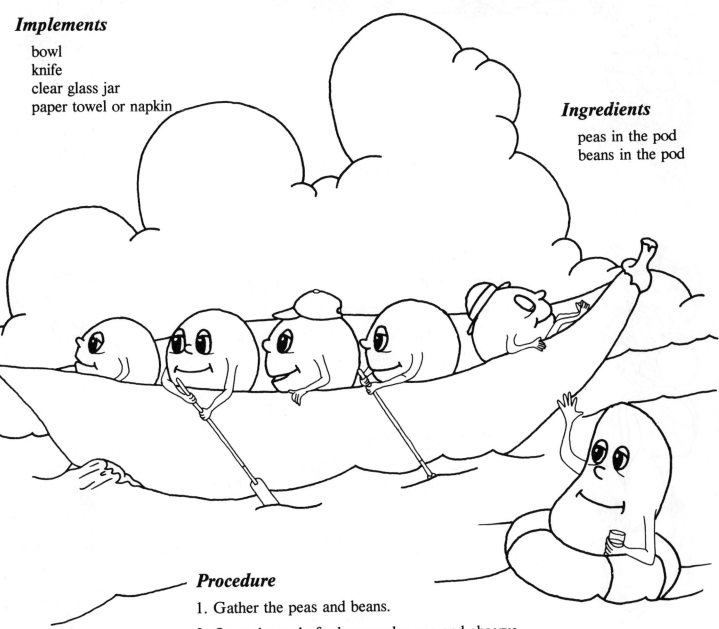

## Procedure

1. Gather the peas and beans.

2. Open the pod of a bean and a pea and observe.

3. Cut a seed in half lengthwise and observe.

4. Dampen a paper towel and wrap it around the inside of the jar.

5. Place whole butter bean seeds between the sides of the glass jar and the paper towel.

6. Keep the paper towel moist at all times.

7. Place the jar in a window sill and watch the seeds grow.

# Vegetable Prints

## Objectives

To provide the opportunity for the child to:

1. Learn a printing process;

2. Learn the shape of various vegetables;

3. Create interesting designs.

## Other Suggestions

Create interesting vegetable prints and add lines to form animals or other figures.

# *Vegetable Prints*

## *Ingredients*

tempera paint or water base printing ink
jars or cups
paper
vegetables

## *Implements*

rubber roller
brush

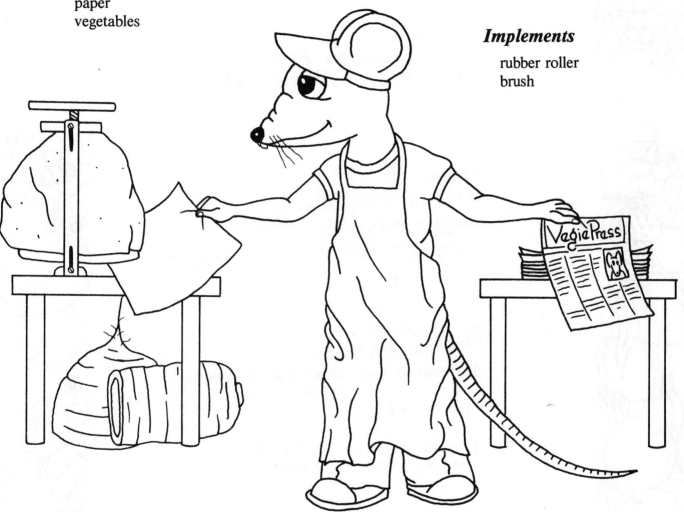

## *Procedure*

1. Gather the rubber roller or brush, tempera paint or printing ink, and paper, jars or cups.

2. Cut designs in the vegetables. You may want to cut vegetables in half first.

3. Dip the vegetable design into a cup of paint.

4. Press the vegetable down on paper or cloth. You may want to press it many times to make a pattern.

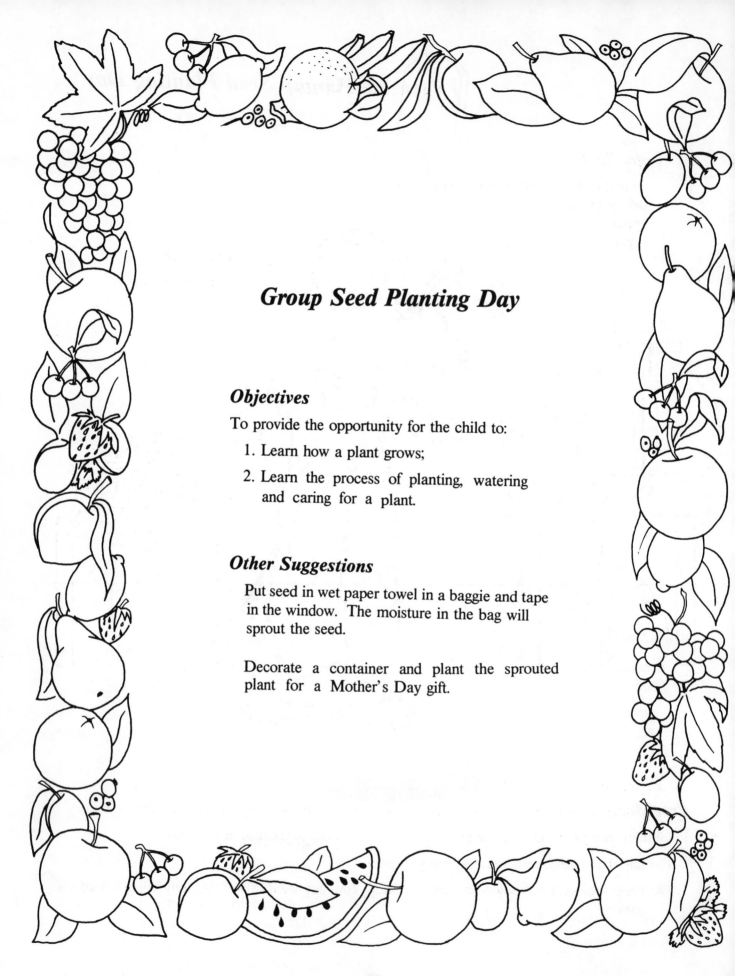

# *Group Seed Planting Day*

## *Objectives*

To provide the opportunity for the child to:

1. Learn how a plant grows;

2. Learn the process of planting, watering and caring for a plant.

## *Other Suggestions*

Put seed in wet paper towel in a baggie and tape in the window. The moisture in the bag will sprout the seed.

Decorate a container and plant the sprouted plant for a Mother's Day gift.

# Group Seed Planting Day

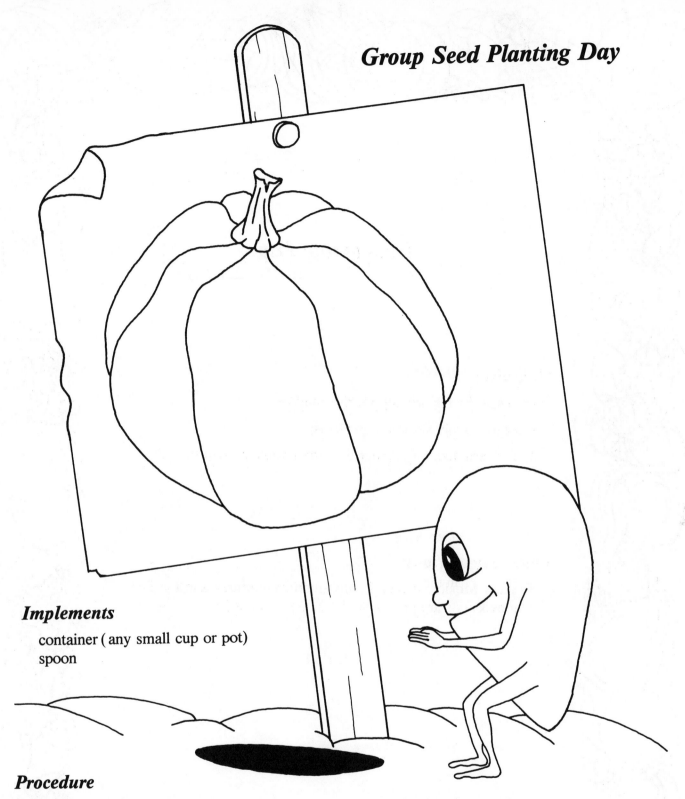

## Implements

container (any small cup or pot)
spoon

## Procedure

1. Gather the seeds.

2. Put dirt in the container.

3. Plant the seed one inch under the top of soil.

4. Water it and put it in a window.

5. Watch it grow.

## Ingredients

packaged seeds
seeds from food: pumpkin, watermelon,
   corn, lima beans, etc.
dirt

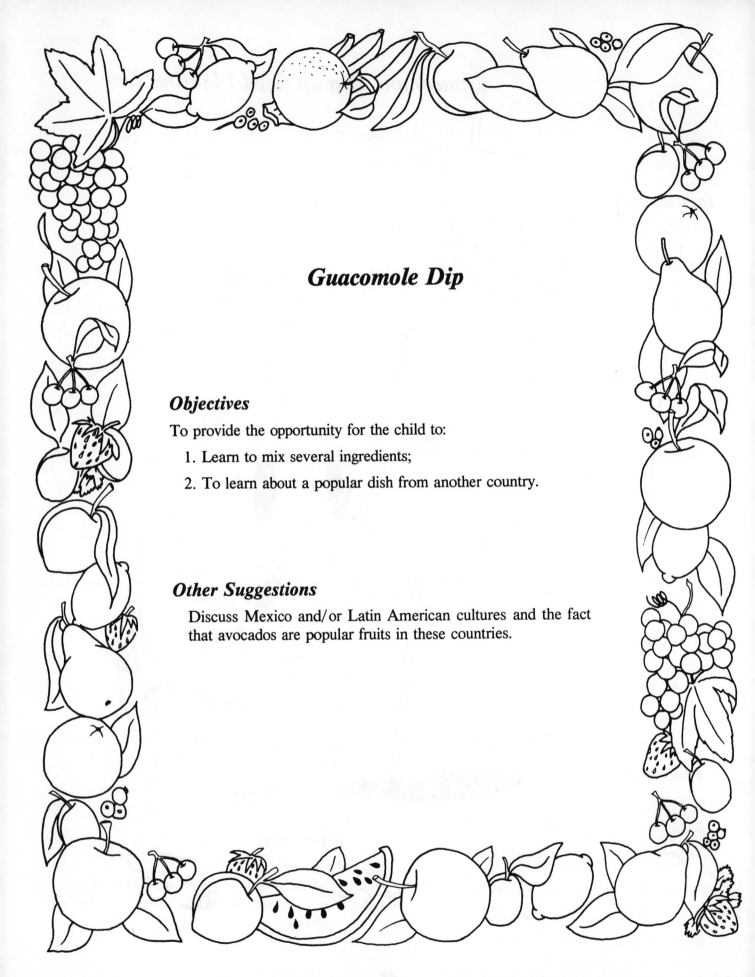

# Guacomole Dip

## Objectives

To provide the opportunity for the child to:

1. Learn to mix several ingredients;

2. To learn about a popular dish from another country.

## Other Suggestions

Discuss Mexico and/or Latin American cultures and the fact that avocados are popular fruits in these countries.

# Guacomole Dip

## Ingredients

2 large avocados — peeled and chopped
1 small can taco sauce (about 4 oz.)
dash of garlic salt
1 T. lemon juice

## Implements

bowl
spoon
knife
blender (or portable hand mixer)

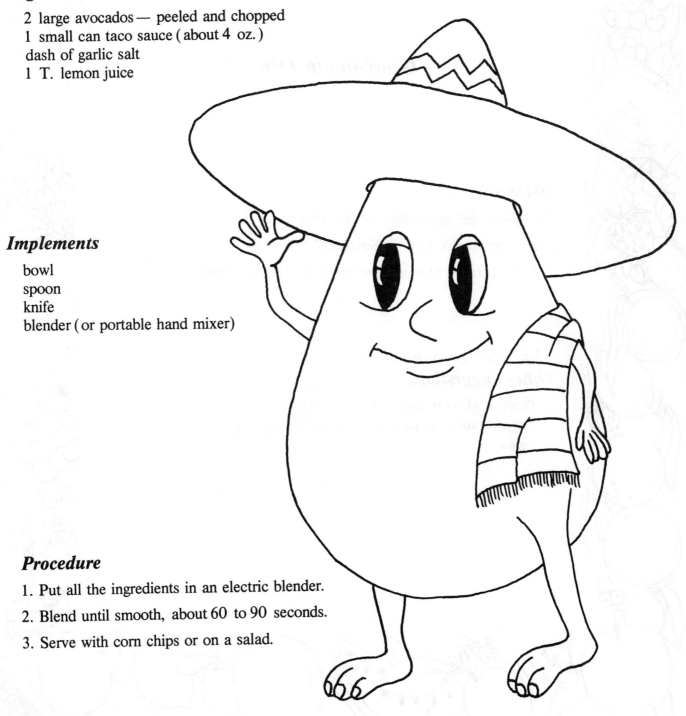

## Procedure

1. Put all the ingredients in an electric blender.

2. Blend until smooth, about 60 to 90 seconds.

3. Serve with corn chips or on a salad.

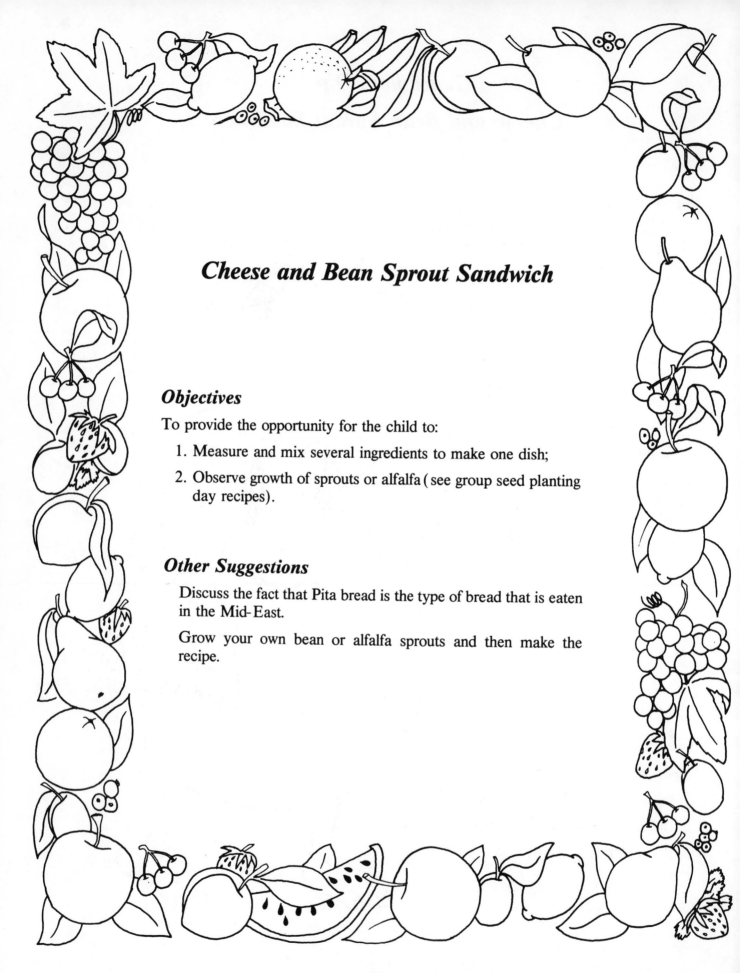

# Cheese and Bean Sprout Sandwich

## Objectives

To provide the opportunity for the child to:

1. Measure and mix several ingredients to make one dish;

2. Observe growth of sprouts or alfalfa (see group seed planting day recipes).

## Other Suggestions

Discuss the fact that Pita bread is the type of bread that is eaten in the Mid-East.

Grow your own bean or alfalfa sprouts and then make the recipe.

# Cheese and Bean Sprout Sandwich

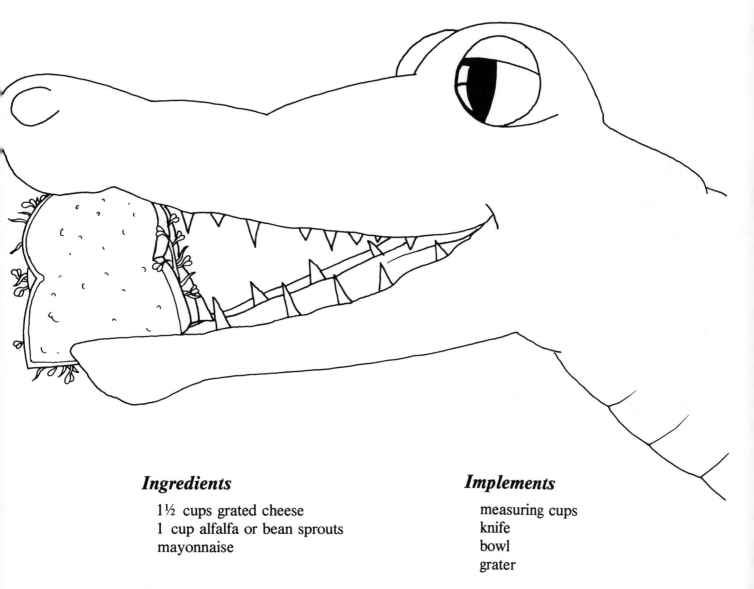

## Ingredients

1½ cups grated cheese
1 cup alfalfa or bean sprouts
mayonnaise

## Implements

measuring cups
knife
bowl
grater

## Procedure

1. Mix up the cheese and sprouts.

2. Add mayonnaise a little at a time until the mixture is as thick as you want it.

3. Spread it on Pita bread, bread or crackers and eat!

# Concept II:

## The Human Being Relates to His Environment Through His Five Senses

*Food Look Alikes*
*Root Vegetables*
*Cucumber Comparisons*
*Fresh Fruit*
*Corn-on-the-Cob*
*Hot Dogs*
*Painted Toast*
*Pigs-in-a-Blanket*
*Pop Corn*
*Cooked Vegetables*
*Five Vegetables*
*Beef Stew*
*Baked Apples*
*Peanut Butter Balls*

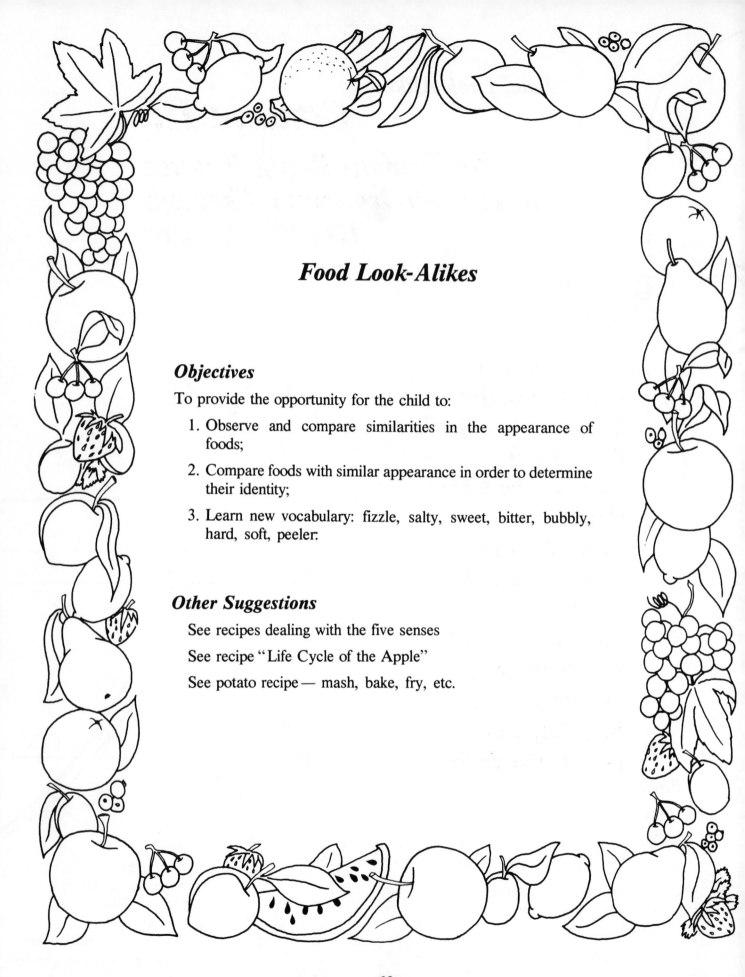

# Food Look-Alikes

## Objectives

To provide the opportunity for the child to:

1. Observe and compare similarities in the appearance of foods;

2. Compare foods with similar appearance in order to determine their identity;

3. Learn new vocabulary: fizzle, salty, sweet, bitter, bubbly, hard, soft, peeler.

## Other Suggestions

See recipes dealing with the five senses

See recipe "Life Cycle of the Apple"

See potato recipe — mash, bake, fry, etc.

# Food Look-Alikes

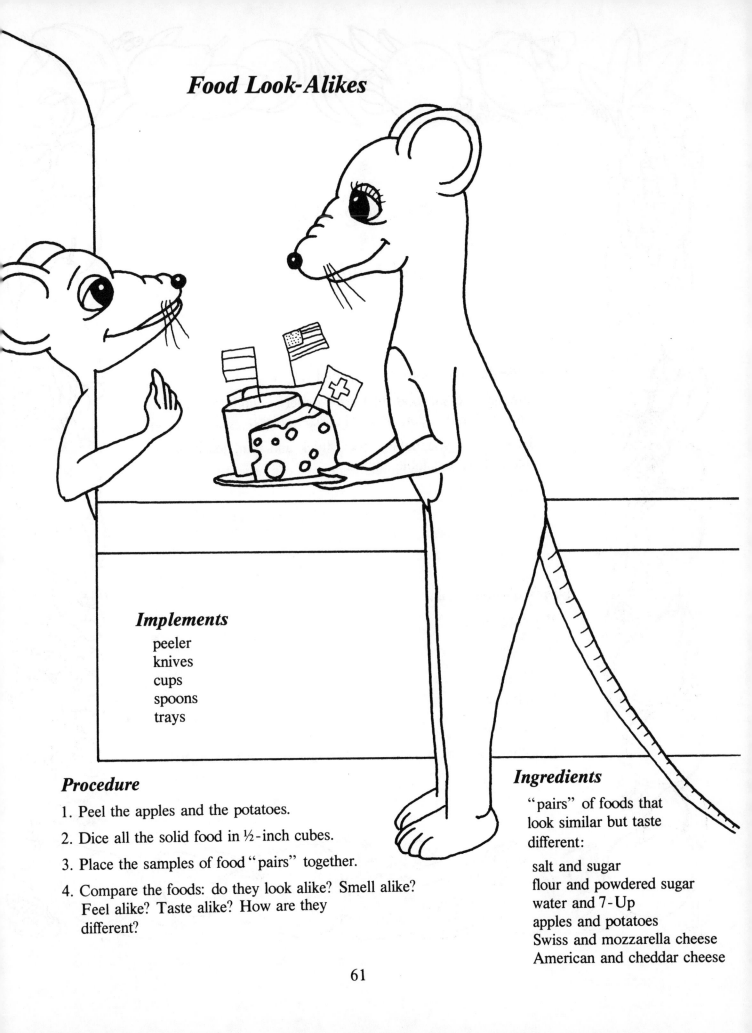

## Implements

peeler
knives
cups
spoons
trays

## Procedure

1. Peel the apples and the potatoes.

2. Dice all the solid food in ½-inch cubes.

3. Place the samples of food "pairs" together.

4. Compare the foods: do they look alike? Smell alike? Feel alike? Taste alike? How are they different?

## Ingredients

"pairs" of foods that look similar but taste different:

salt and sugar
flour and powdered sugar
water and 7-Up
apples and potatoes
Swiss and mozzarella cheese
American and cheddar cheese

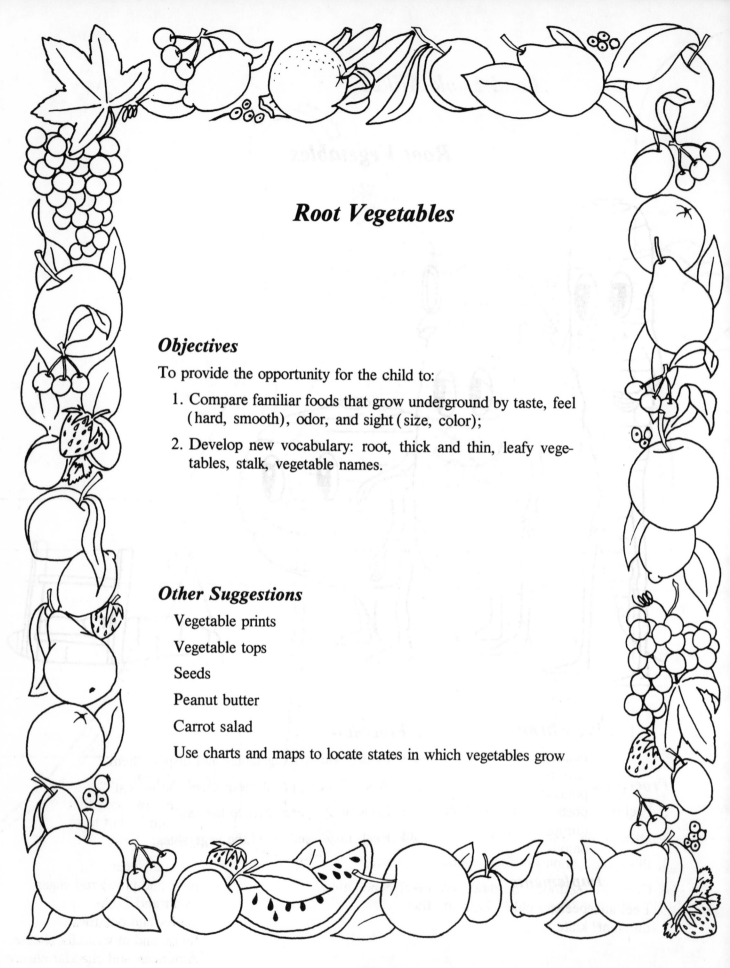

# Root Vegetables

## Objectives

To provide the opportunity for the child to:

1. Compare familiar foods that grow underground by taste, feel (hard, smooth), odor, and sight (size, color);

2. Develop new vocabulary: root, thick and thin, leafy vegetables, stalk, vegetable names.

## Other Suggestions

Vegetable prints

Vegetable tops

Seeds

Peanut butter

Carrot salad

Use charts and maps to locate states in which vegetables grow

# Root Vegetables

## Ingredients

peanuts
carrots
potatoes
beets
turnips
onions

## Implements

peeler
knife

## Procedure

1. Collect various vegetables and display them.

2. Ask "Which part of these plants do we eat?"

3. Look at the vegetables in the raw.

4. Feel, taste, and smell the vegetables.

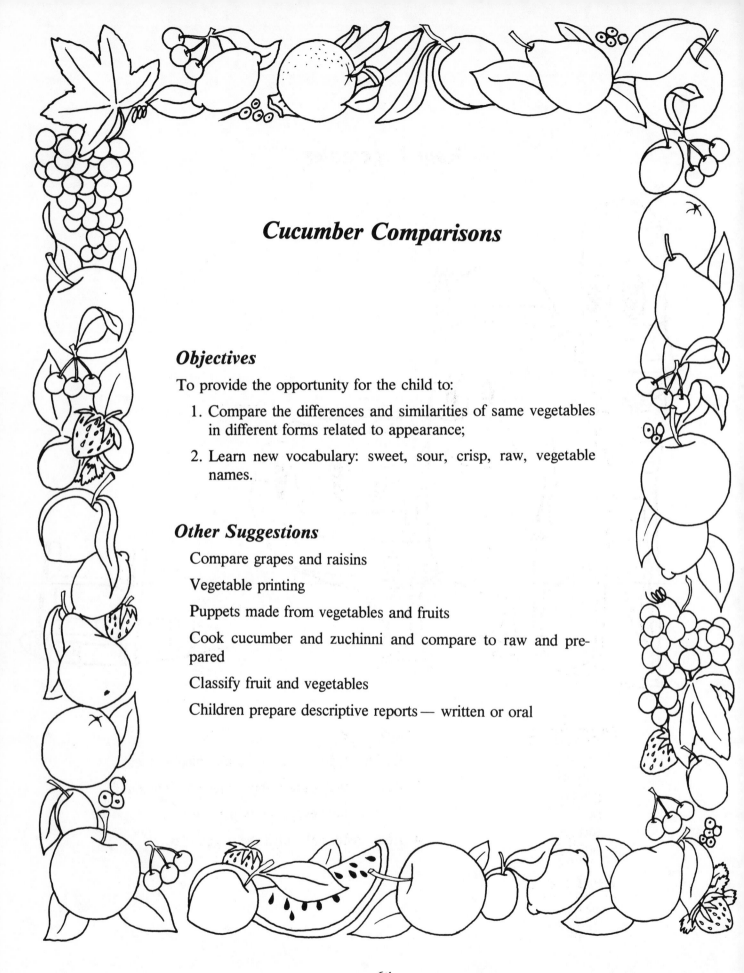

# Cucumber Comparisons

## Objectives

To provide the opportunity for the child to:

1. Compare the differences and similarities of same vegetables in different forms related to appearance;

2. Learn new vocabulary: sweet, sour, crisp, raw, vegetable names.

## Other Suggestions

Compare grapes and raisins

Vegetable printing

Puppets made from vegetables and fruits

Cook cucumber and zuchinni and compare to raw and pre-pared

Classify fruit and vegetables

Children prepare descriptive reports — written or oral

# Cucumber Comparisons

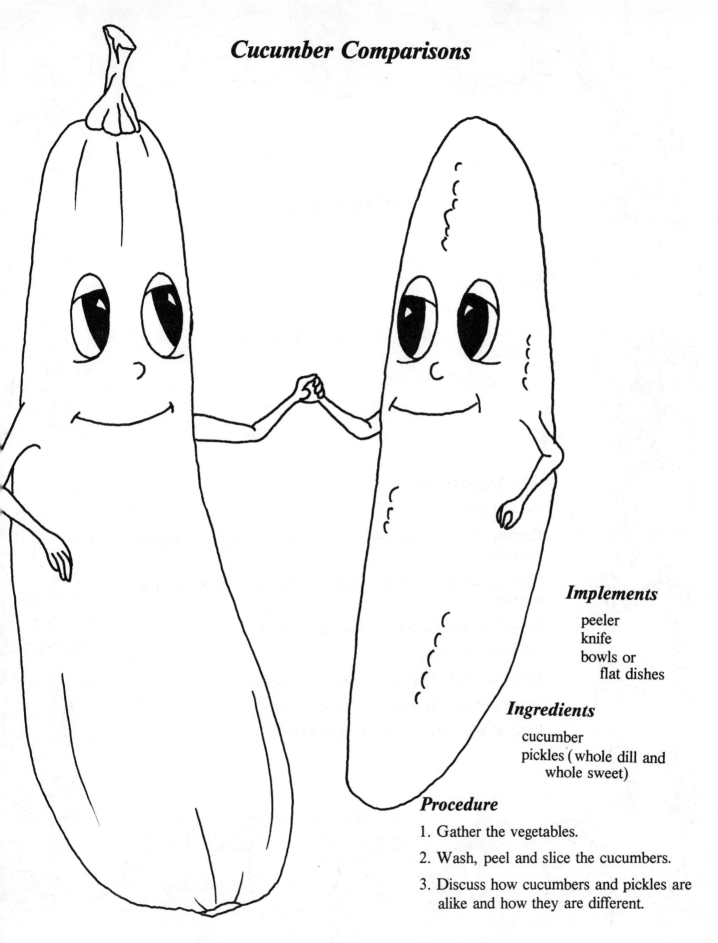

### Implements

    peeler
    knife
    bowls or
       flat dishes

### Ingredients

    cucumber
    pickles (whole dill and
       whole sweet)

### Procedure

1. Gather the vegetables.

2. Wash, peel and slice the cucumbers.

3. Discuss how cucumbers and pickles are alike and how they are different.

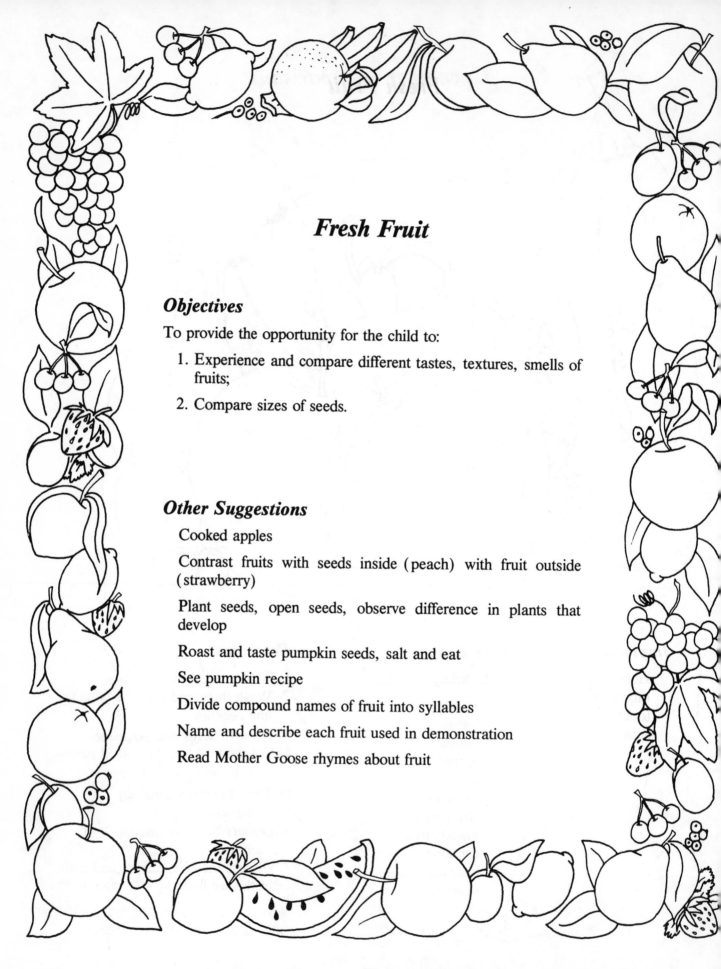

# Fresh Fruit

## Objectives

To provide the opportunity for the child to:

1. Experience and compare different tastes, textures, smells of fruits;

2. Compare sizes of seeds.

## Other Suggestions

Cooked apples

Contrast fruits with seeds inside (peach) with fruit outside (strawberry)

Plant seeds, open seeds, observe difference in plants that develop

Roast and taste pumpkin seeds, salt and eat

See pumpkin recipe

Divide compound names of fruit into syllables

Name and describe each fruit used in demonstration

Read Mother Goose rhymes about fruit

# Fresh Fruit

## Implements

knife
mixing bowl
toothpicks
small cups

## Ingredients

A variety of fruits:

    peaches
    bananas
    plums
    apples
    grapes
    pineapple
    strawberries
    blackberries
    cantelope
    honeydew melon
    watermelon

## Procedure

1. Gather the various fruits.
2. Wash them and peel the bananas and peaches.
3. Remove seeds and set aside.
4. Cut the fruit into bite-sized pieces and divide into small cups.
5. Taste the fruits using the toothpicks.
6. Discuss the taste and smell of each fruit.
7. Discuss the size, shape, and color of the seeds.

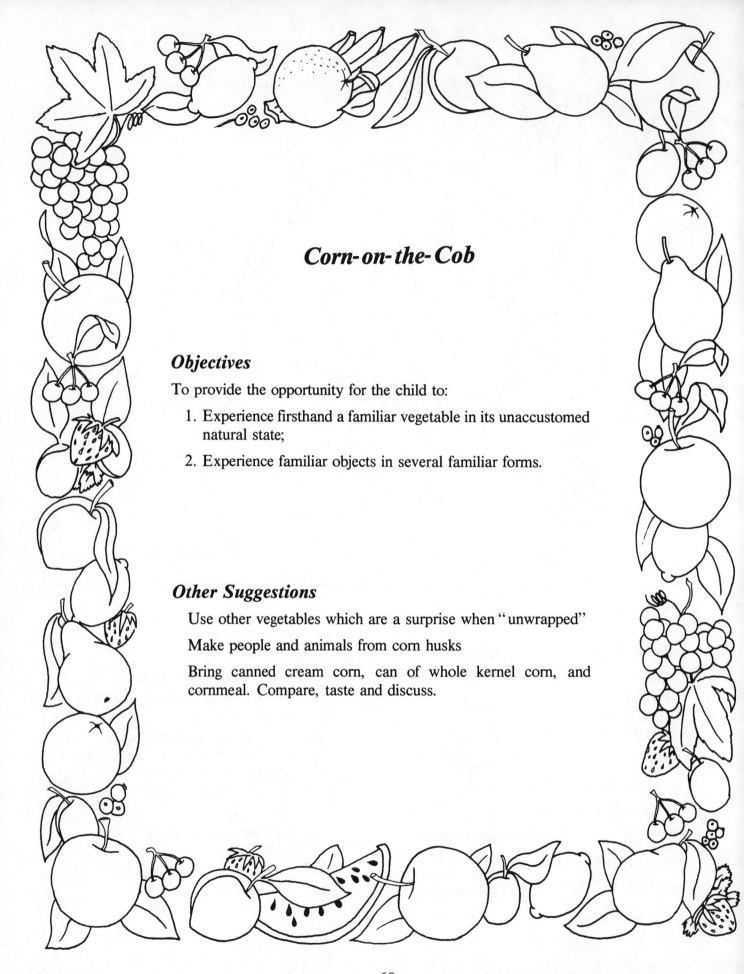

# Corn-on-the-Cob

## Objectives

To provide the opportunity for the child to:

1. Experience firsthand a familiar vegetable in its unaccustomed natural state;

2. Experience familiar objects in several familiar forms.

## Other Suggestions

Use other vegetables which are a surprise when "unwrapped"

Make people and animals from corn husks

Bring canned cream corn, can of whole kernel corn, and cornmeal. Compare, taste and discuss.

# Corn-on-the-Cob

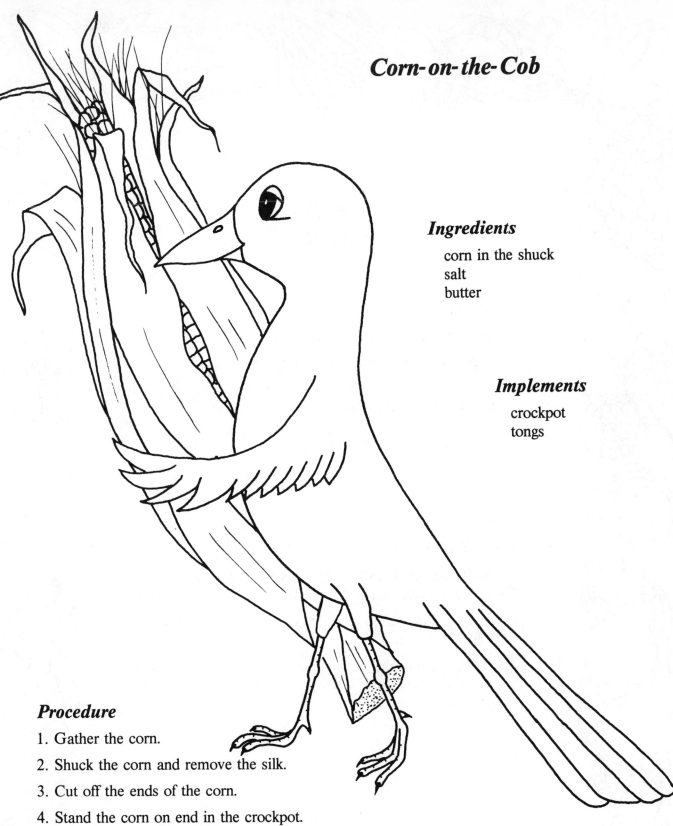

## Ingredients

corn in the shuck
salt
butter

## Implements

crockpot
tongs

## Procedure

1. Gather the corn.

2. Shuck the corn and remove the silk.

3. Cut off the ends of the corn.

4. Stand the corn on end in the crockpot.

5. Cover the corn with water.

6. Cover the pot and cook on high until the corn is tender.

7. Use tongs to remove the corn. Add butter and salt, and eat!

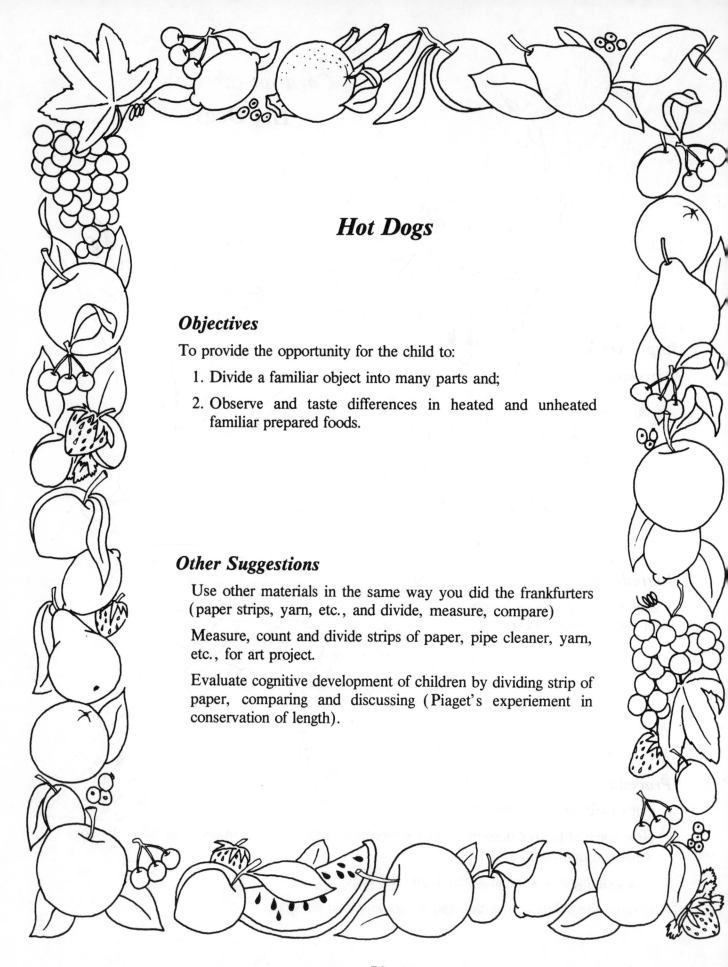

# Hot Dogs

## Objectives

To provide the opportunity for the child to:

1. Divide a familiar object into many parts and;

2. Observe and taste differences in heated and unheated familiar prepared foods.

## Other Suggestions

Use other materials in the same way you did the frankfurters (paper strips, yarn, etc., and divide, measure, compare)

Measure, count and divide strips of paper, pipe cleaner, yarn, etc., for art project.

Evaluate cognitive development of children by dividing strip of paper, comparing and discussing (Piaget's experiement in conservation of length).

# Hot Dogs

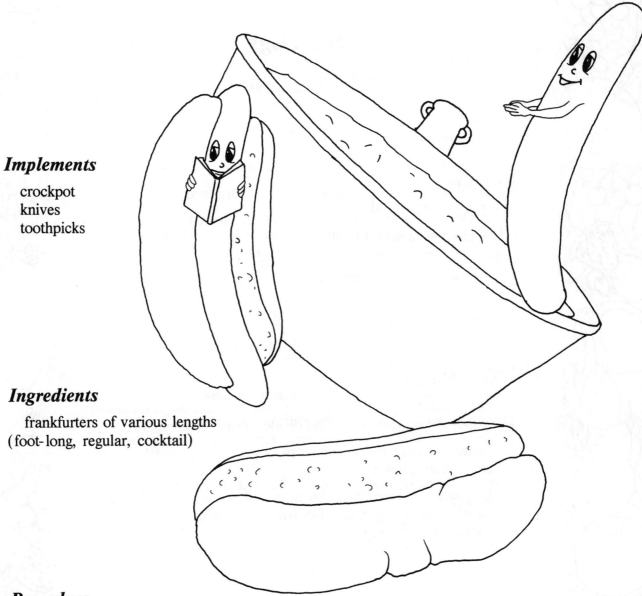

## Implements

crockpot
knives
toothpicks

## Ingredients

frankfurters of various lengths
(foot-long, regular, cocktail)

## Procedure

1. Cut various lengths of hot dogs.

2. Heat some of the hot dogs in a crock pot on high with no water. In about an hour, the dogs will begin to brown.

3. Use toothpicks to sample hot and cold hot dogs.

4. Discuss the differences in the taste of hot and cold hot dogs.

# Painted Toast

## Objectives

To provide the opportunity for the child to:

1. Observe changes in milk and in familiar foods when heat is applied (effects of heat on familiar foods);

2. Observe changes brought about in familiar foods by addition of a coloring agent.

## Other Suggestions

Add flavoring to colored milk to compare changes in taste

Discuss differences in painting with colored milk and regular paints — why you cannot eat paint and you can eat colored milk

Write a poem describing colored painted toast, taste, look, odor, texture.

# Painted Toast

## Ingredients

bread (white)
milk
food coloring

## Implements

toaster oven
small jars
plastic knives
pastry brush or new paint brushes

## Procedure

1. Tint jars of milk with food coloring.

2. Paint the bread with milk using pastry brushes.

3. Put the bread in the toaster oven.

4. Take it out when it is brown and crisp and taste.

# Pigs-in-a-Blanket

## Objectives

To provide the opportunity for the child to:

1. Observe changes from uncooked to cooked state of a familiar food;

2. Prepare two familiar foods in a unique way;

3. Observe and taste difference between cooked and uncooked state of a familiar food;

4. Observe changes in texture and appearance caused when heat is applied to a familiar food.

## Other Suggestions

Prepare pigs-in-a-blanket for a field trip or picnic.

May add cheese and/or bacon; observe changes to these foods.

Discuss familiar settings for eating hot dogs (picnics, ball games, cook-outs, camping, Boy Scouts, etc.)

# Pigs-in-a-Blanket

## Ingredients

hot dogs (or vienna sausages)
canned biscuits

## Implements

toaster oven
toothpicks
plastic knives

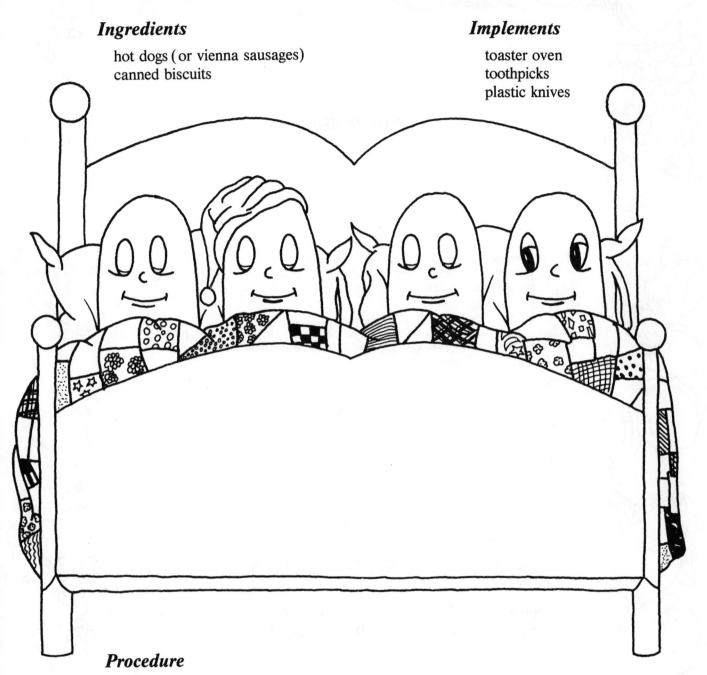

## Procedure

1. Flatten each biscuit and wrap it around a hot dog.

2. Squeeze the dough together or stick it with toothpicks to prevent unwinding.

3. Bake according to directions on biscuit package (approximately 10 minutes).

# Popcorn

## Objectives

To provide the opportunity for the child to:

1. Use all five senses in observing changes when heat is applied to a familiar food;

2. Contrast color changes in color of popcorn, a familiar food, as it changes from seed state to edible state.

## Other Suggestions

Other kinds of corn

Discuss where we usually eat popcorn

Write description of changes in popcorn; create explanations

Describe how popcorn kernel feels as it changes when heat is applied to it.

Use popped popcorn for craft collage, etc. Make strings of popcorn for Christmas tree, outdoor tree for birds.

# Popcorn

## Ingredients

popcorn
cooking oil
salt

## Implements

Popcorn popper or electric skillet

## Procedure

1. Cover bottom of corn popper with oil (about 2 T. of oil for each ½ cup of raw popcorn).

2. Add popcorn and cover.

3. Cook until popping stops.

4. Add salt and/or buttery seasoning.

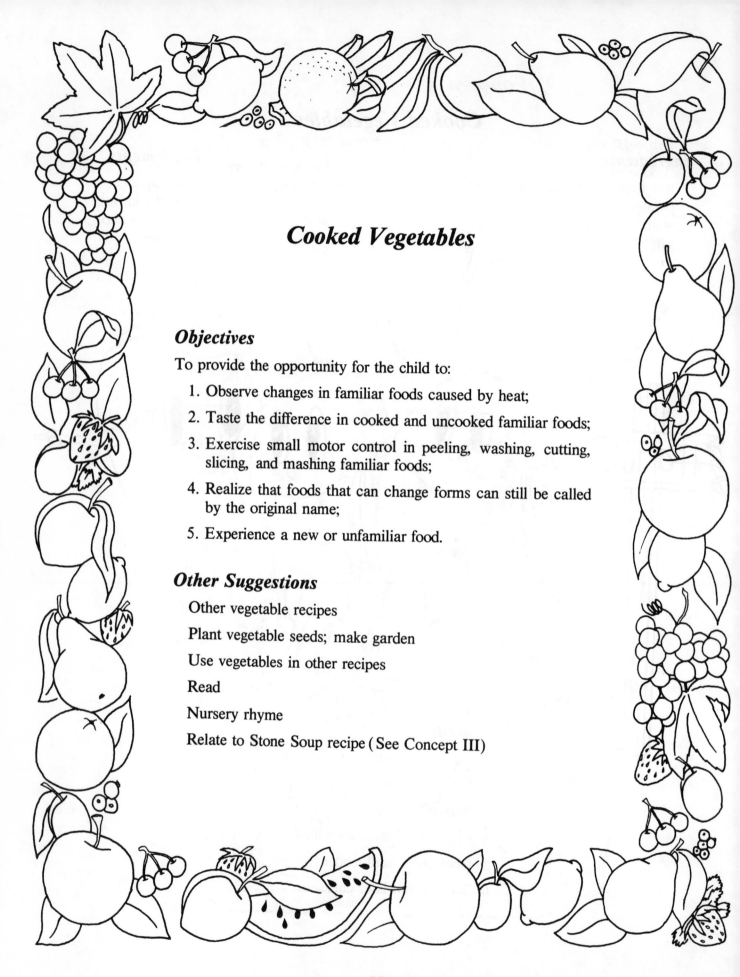

# Cooked Vegetables

## Objectives

To provide the opportunity for the child to:

1. Observe changes in familiar foods caused by heat;

2. Taste the difference in cooked and uncooked familiar foods;

3. Exercise small motor control in peeling, washing, cutting, slicing, and mashing familiar foods;

4. Realize that foods that can change forms can still be called by the original name;

5. Experience a new or unfamiliar food.

## Other Suggestions

Other vegetable recipes

Plant vegetable seeds; make garden

Use vegetables in other recipes

Read

Nursery rhyme

Relate to Stone Soup recipe (See Concept III)

# Cooked Vegetables

## Ingredients

raw fresh vegetables: squash, onions,
potatoes, corn, etc.
water
salt

## Implements

crockpot
plastic knives
bowls or cups
spoons

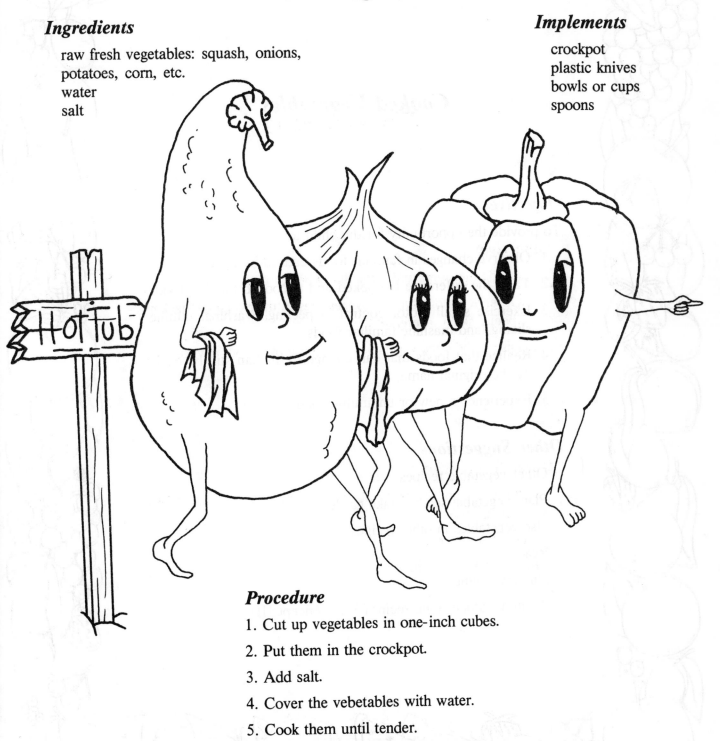

## Procedure

1. Cut up vegetables in one-inch cubes.

2. Put them in the crockpot.

3. Add salt.

4. Cover the vebetables with water.

5. Cook them until tender.

6. Serve in bowls or cups.

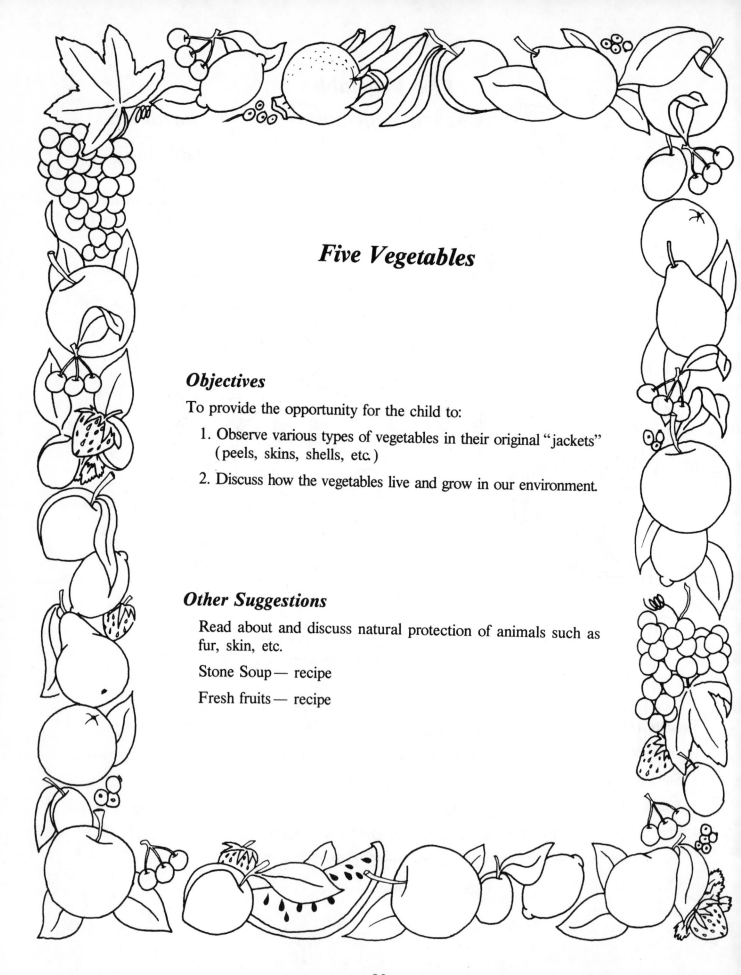

# Five Vegetables

## Objectives

To provide the opportunity for the child to:

1. Observe various types of vegetables in their original "jackets" (peels, skins, shells, etc.)

2. Discuss how the vegetables live and grow in our environment.

## Other Suggestions

Read about and discuss natural protection of animals such as fur, skin, etc.

Stone Soup — recipe

Fresh fruits — recipe

# *Five Vegetables*

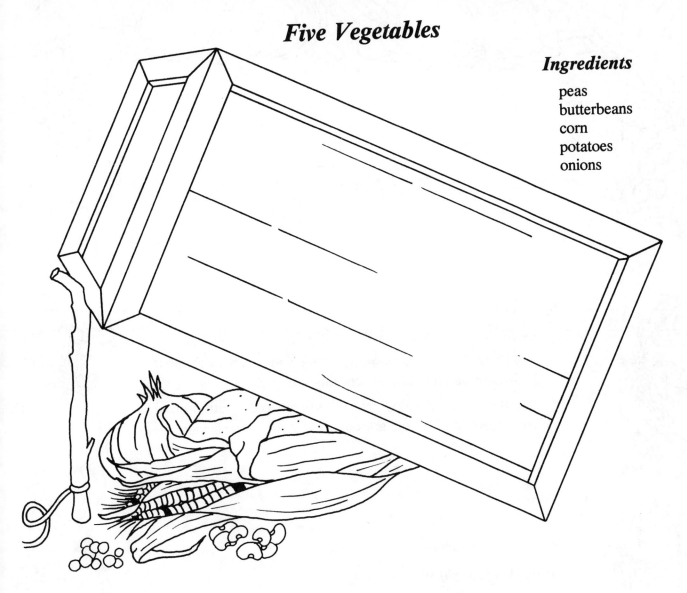

## *Ingredients*

peas
butterbeans
corn
potatoes
onions

## *Implements*

peeler
plastic knife
crockpot (if you desire to cook the vegetables)
bowls
spoons

## *Procedure*

1. Observe the vegetables in their "wrapping."

2. Shell the peas and butterbeans.

3. Shuck the corn and remove the silk.

4. Peel the potatoes and onions.

5. Put vegetables in the crockpot, add salt, and cover the vegetables with water.

6. Cook until tender.

7. Serve in bowls.

# Beef Stew

## Objectives

To provide the opportunity for the child to:

1. Differentitate taste, appearance, feel and smell of familiar foods both before and after cooking;

2. Experience the fact that some foods are good both cooked and uncooked — others are not.

## Other Suggestions

Discuss origins of foods in stew

Read *Stone Soup* and relate to that recipe.

# Beef Stew

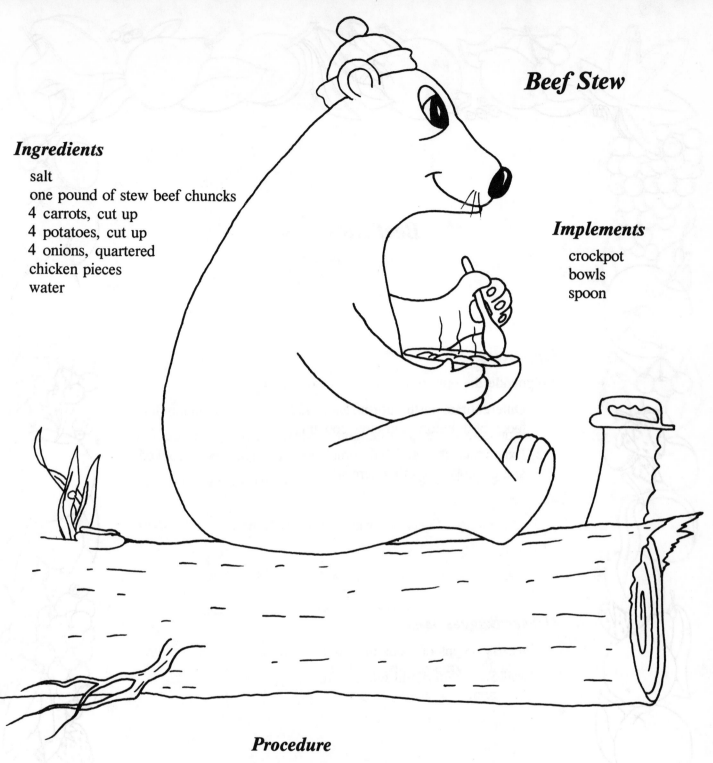

## Ingredients

salt
one pound of stew beef chuncks
4 carrots, cut up
4 potatoes, cut up
4 onions, quartered
chicken pieces
water

## Implements

crockpot
bowls
spoon

## Procedure

1. Cut beef and vegetables in bite-sized pieces.

2. Place in crockpot.

3. Add salt.

4. Cover with water.

5. Cook until tender.

6. Serve in bowls.

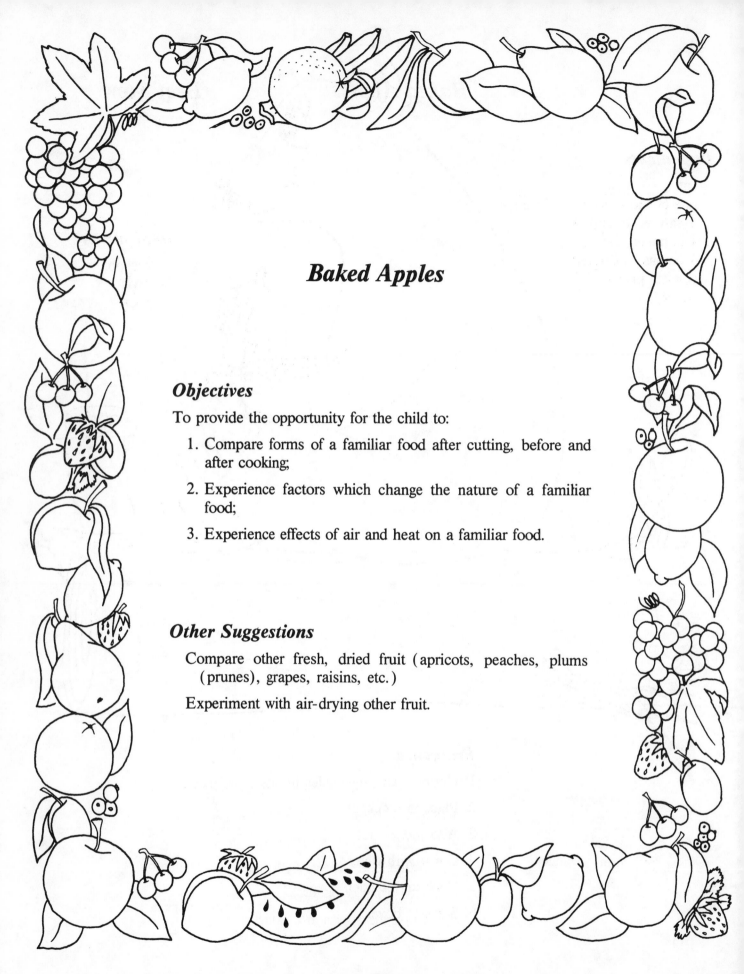

# Baked Apples

## Objectives

To provide the opportunity for the child to:

1. Compare forms of a familiar food after cutting, before and after cooking;

2. Experience factors which change the nature of a familiar food;

3. Experience effects of air and heat on a familiar food.

## Other Suggestions

Compare other fresh, dried fruit (apricots, peaches, plums (prunes), grapes, raisins, etc.)

Experiment with air-drying other fruit.

# Baked Apples

## Ingredients

fresh apples
raisins
sugar
cinnamon
butter

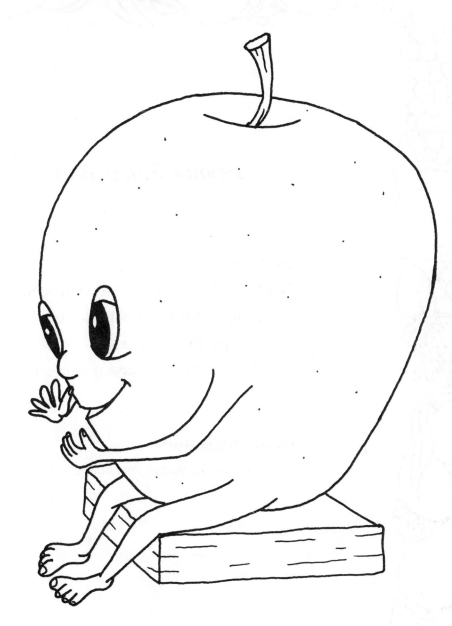

## Implements

electric skillet
plastic knives
corer or peeler

## Procedure

1. Wash the apples.

2. Core the apples.

3. Fill the apples with raisins.

4. Sprinkle the apples with sugar and cinnamon.

5. Add a pat of butter.

6. Cook the apples in a skillet until tender.

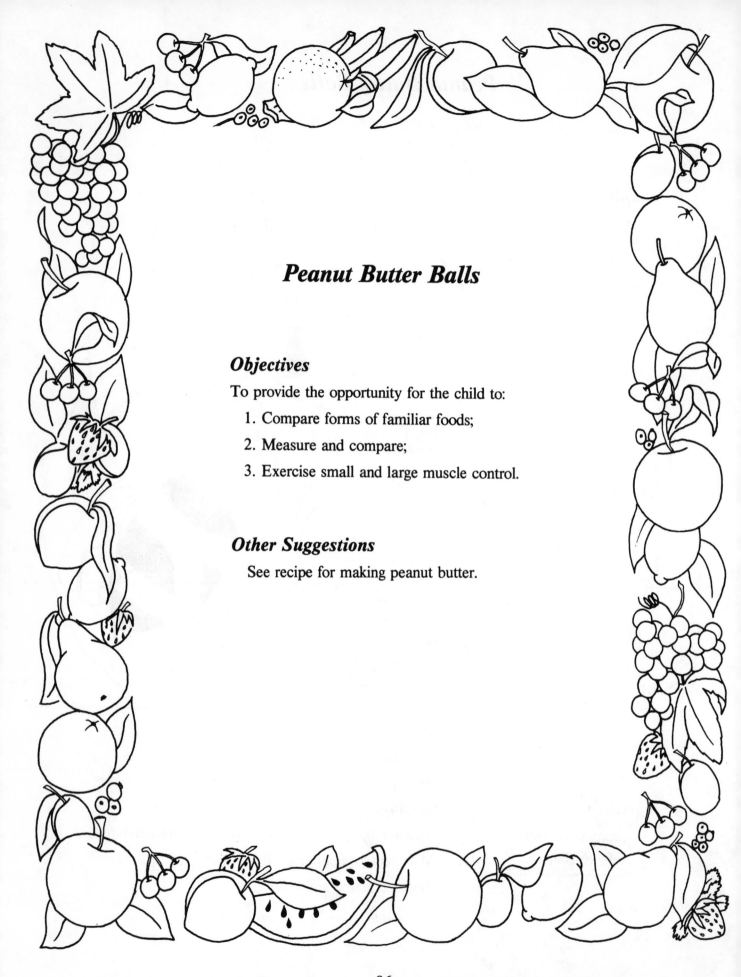

# Peanut Butter Balls

## Objectives

To provide the opportunity for the child to:

1. Compare forms of familiar foods;

2. Measure and compare;

3. Exercise small and large muscle control.

## Other Suggestions

See recipe for making peanut butter.

# Peanut Butter Balls

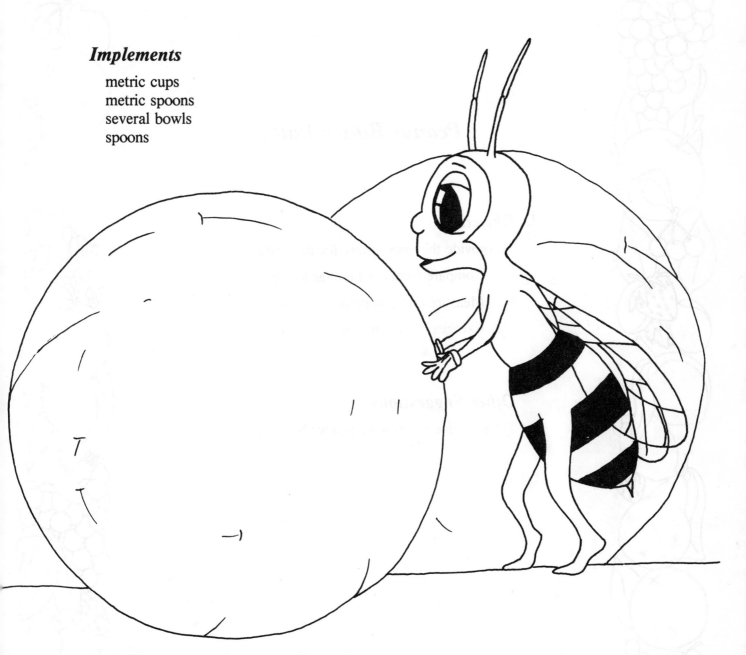

## Implements

metric cups
metric spoons
several bowls
spoons

## Ingredients

½ cup peanut butter
¼ cup honey
2 cups powdered milk

## Procedure

1. Measure the peanut butter, honey and powdered milk.

2. Mix them together and roll into balls.

3. Place on platter and serve.

# Concept III:

## Energy is Necessary for Life and for All Living Things to Interact with Their Environment

*Butter*
*Fruit-Ade Juice*
*Banana Pudding*
*Thick Milk Shakes*
*Fruit Ice*
*Fruit Comparisons*
*Cheese Biscuits*
*Cheese Soup*
*Peanut Butter*
*Cheese Confetti*
*Stone Soup*
*Whole Egg Mayonnaise*
*Ice Cream*
*Juice Popsicles*
*Cinnamon-Sugar Toast*
*Jello*
*Fruit Butter*
*Pizza*
*Eggs*
*Rainbow Cake*
*Cornbread*
*Tuna Salad*
*Chunk Style Applesauce*

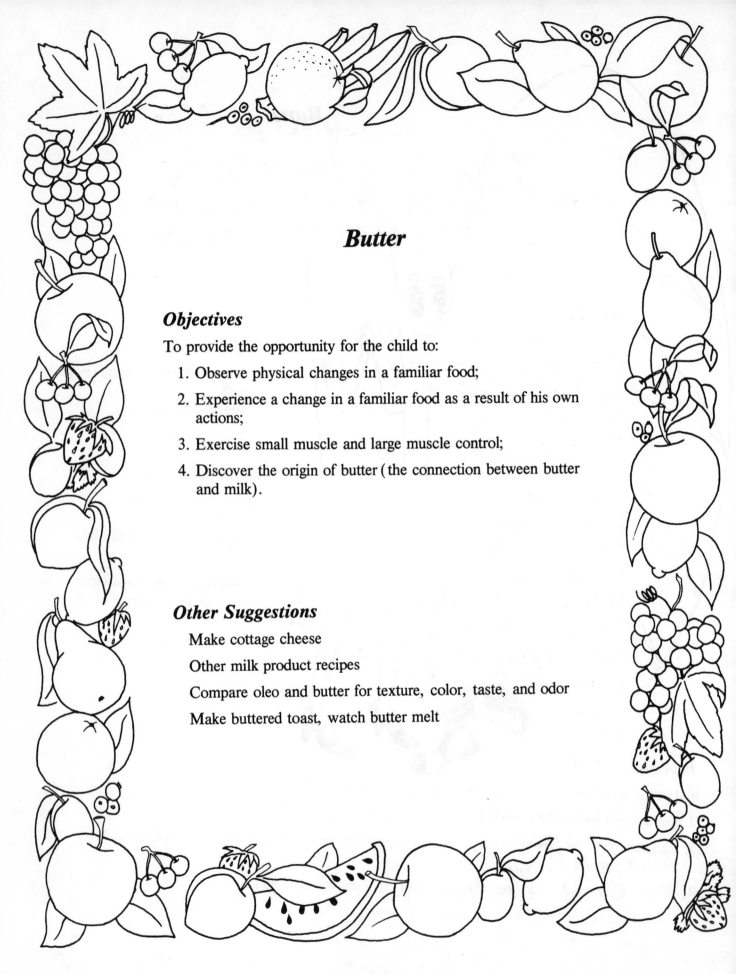

# Butter

## Objectives

To provide the opportunity for the child to:

1. Observe physical changes in a familiar food;

2. Experience a change in a familiar food as a result of his own actions;

3. Exercise small muscle and large muscle control;

4. Discover the origin of butter (the connection between butter and milk).

## Other Suggestions

Make cottage cheese

Other milk product recipes

Compare oleo and butter for texture, color, taste, and odor

Make buttered toast, watch butter melt

# Butter

## Ingredients

heavy whipping cream (½ pint)
salt
bread or crackers

## Implements

glass jars with lids
   or
plastic cups with tight lids
   or
wooden churns (available
   from local dairy)

## Procedure

1. Let the cream sit out of the refrigerator for a couple of hours.

2. Put a small amount of cream in each jar and put the lid on tightly.

3. Children shake the jars vigorously, checking frequently for evidence of changes (approximately 20 to 30 minutes).

4. When butter has formed, remove the butter from the liquid, then salt.

5. Spread the butter on bread or crackers and taste.

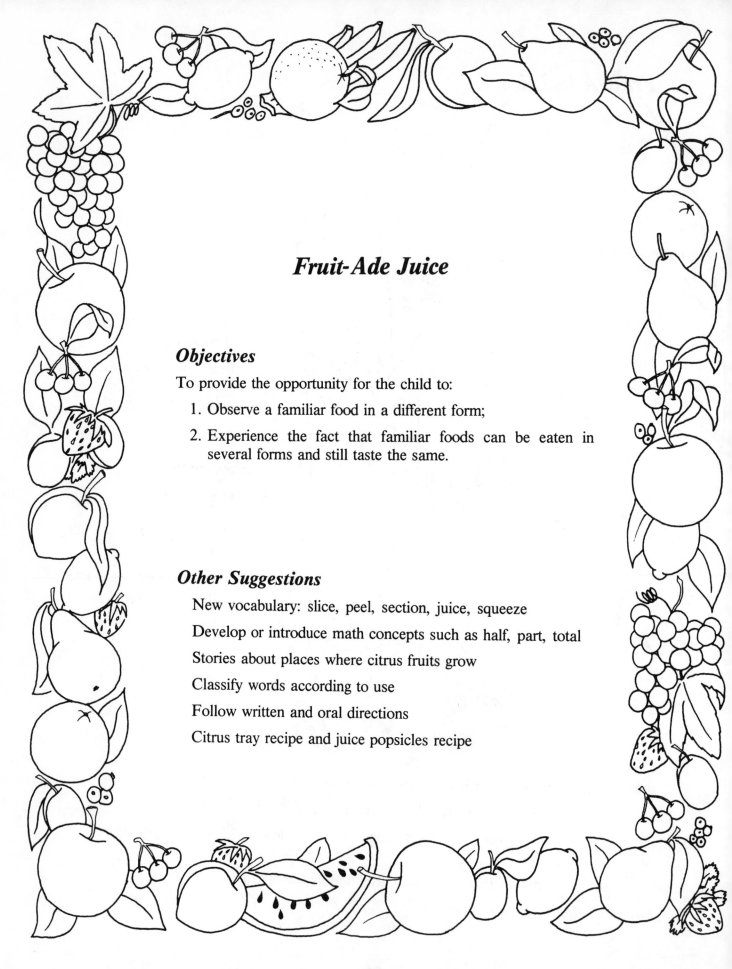

# Fruit-Ade Juice

## Objectives

To provide the opportunity for the child to:

1. Observe a familiar food in a different form;

2. Experience the fact that familiar foods can be eaten in several forms and still taste the same.

## Other Suggestions

New vocabulary: slice, peel, section, juice, squeeze

Develop or introduce math concepts such as half, part, total

Stories about places where citrus fruits grow

Classify words according to use

Follow written and oral directions

Citrus tray recipe and juice popsicles recipe

# Fruit-Ade Juice

**Ingredients**

citrus fruit:

oranges
grapefruits
lemon
lime
( sugar or salt optional )

**Implements**

plastic knife
juicer
pitcher
paper cups

**Procedure**

1. Assemble the fruit.

2. Cut each fruit in half.

3. Squeeze it on a juicer.

4. Pour the juice into the pitcher and taste.

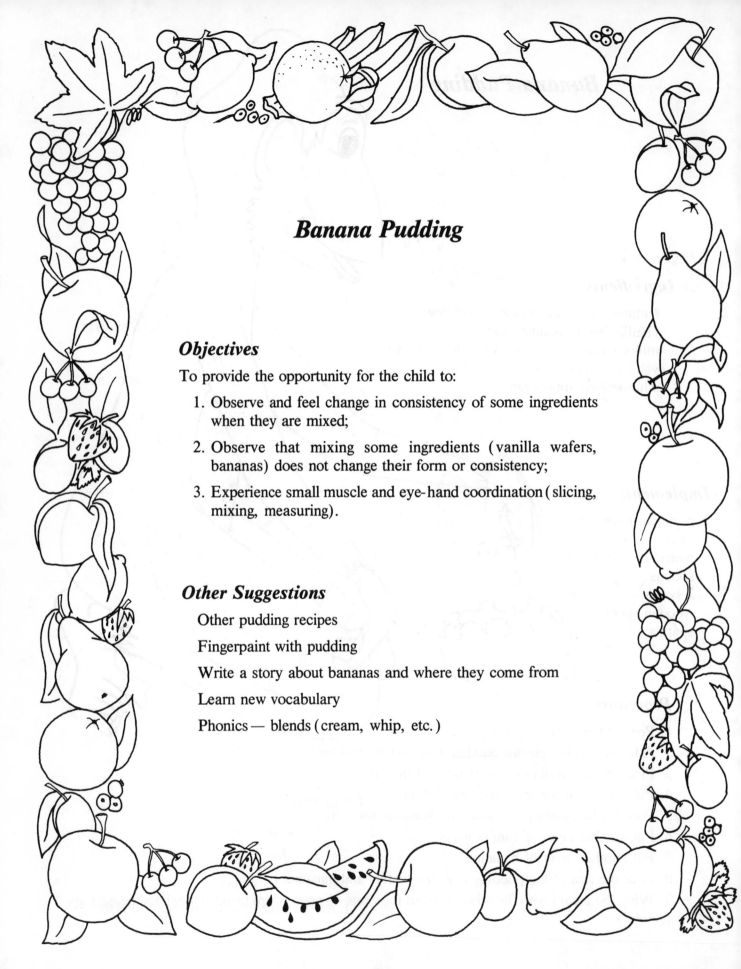

# Banana Pudding

## Objectives

To provide the opportunity for the child to:

1. Observe and feel change in consistency of some ingredients when they are mixed;

2. Observe that mixing some ingredients (vanilla wafers, bananas) does not change their form or consistency;

3. Experience small muscle and eye-hand coordination (slicing, mixing, measuring).

## Other Suggestions

Other pudding recipes

Fingerpaint with pudding

Write a story about bananas and where they come from

Learn new vocabulary

Phonics — blends (cream, whip, etc.)

# Banana Pudding

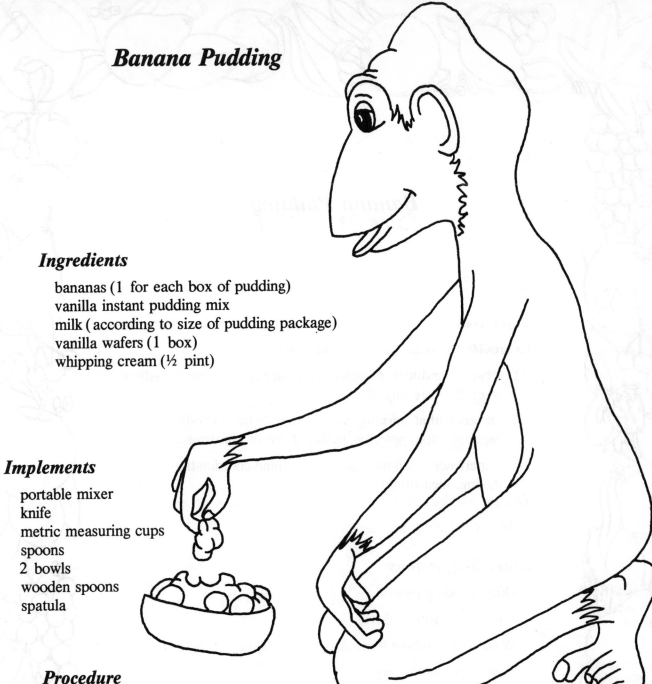

## Ingredients

bananas (1 for each box of pudding)
vanilla instant pudding mix
milk (according to size of pudding package)
vanilla wafers (1 box)
whipping cream (½ pint)

## Implements

portable mixer
knife
metric measuring cups
spoons
2 bowls
wooden spoons
spatula

## Procedure

1. Peel and slice the bananas.
2. Add milk to the instant pudding mix and set this aside.
3. Place vanilla wafers in the bottom of the other bowl.
4. Put a layer of bananas over the wafers.
5. Pour ½ the pudding mix over the bananas and wafers.
6. Put another layer of vanilla wafers.
7. Put another layer of bananas.
8. Pour the rest of the pudding over the wafers and bananas.
9. Whip the cream with the mixer and put it on top. (Cream whips faster if bowl and beaters are cold.).

# Thick Milk Shakes

## Objectives

To provide the opportunity for the child to:

1. Observe a change in food when a whipping process is applied to something cold;

2. Discover the origin of milk shakes.

## Other Suggestions

Plan class party and serve shakes.

# Thick Milk Shakes

## Ingredients

1½ cups milk
⅓ cup chocolate syrup
1 pint vanilla or chocolate
    ice cream

## Implements

blender
individual cups

## Procedure

1. Measure the milk and syrup.

2. Put the milk and syrup in the blender and whip briefly.

3. Stop the blender and add the ice cream, spooning it in the blender in about 8 pieces.

4. Cover the blender and process at whip for about 3 minutes.

5. Pour into cups and serve at once.

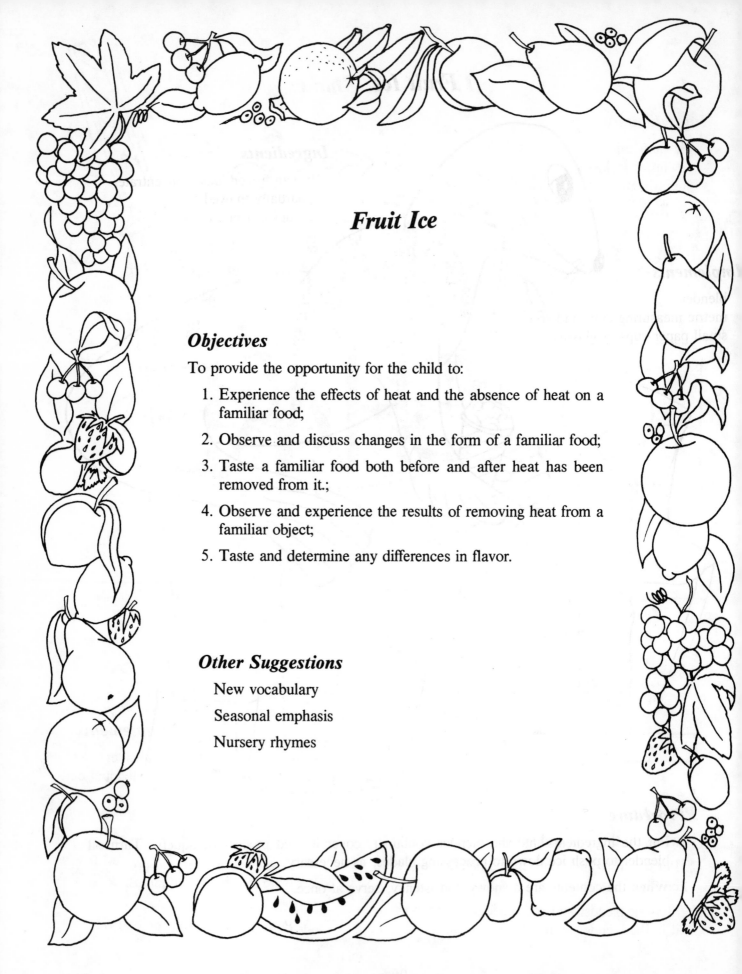

# Fruit Ice

## Objectives

To provide the opportunity for the child to:

1. Experience the effects of heat and the absence of heat on a familiar food;

2. Observe and discuss changes in the form of a familiar food;

3. Taste a familiar food both before and after heat has been removed from it.;

4. Observe and experience the results of removing heat from a familiar object;

5. Taste and determine any differences in flavor.

## Other Suggestions

New vocabulary

Seasonal emphasis

Nursery rhymes

# Fruit Ice

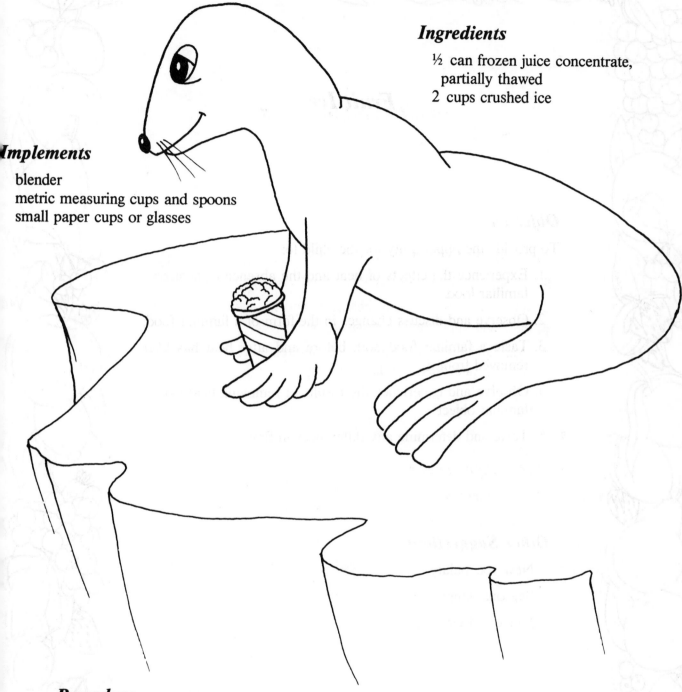

### Ingredients

½ can frozen juice concentrate,
  partially thawed
2 cups crushed ice

### Implements

blender
metric measuring cups and spoons
small paper cups or glasses

### Procedure

1. Put the ingredients into the blender container, cover it, and process at liquefy. Turn off blender to push ice down to processing blades, as necessary.

2. When the contents are a snowy consistency, serve at once.

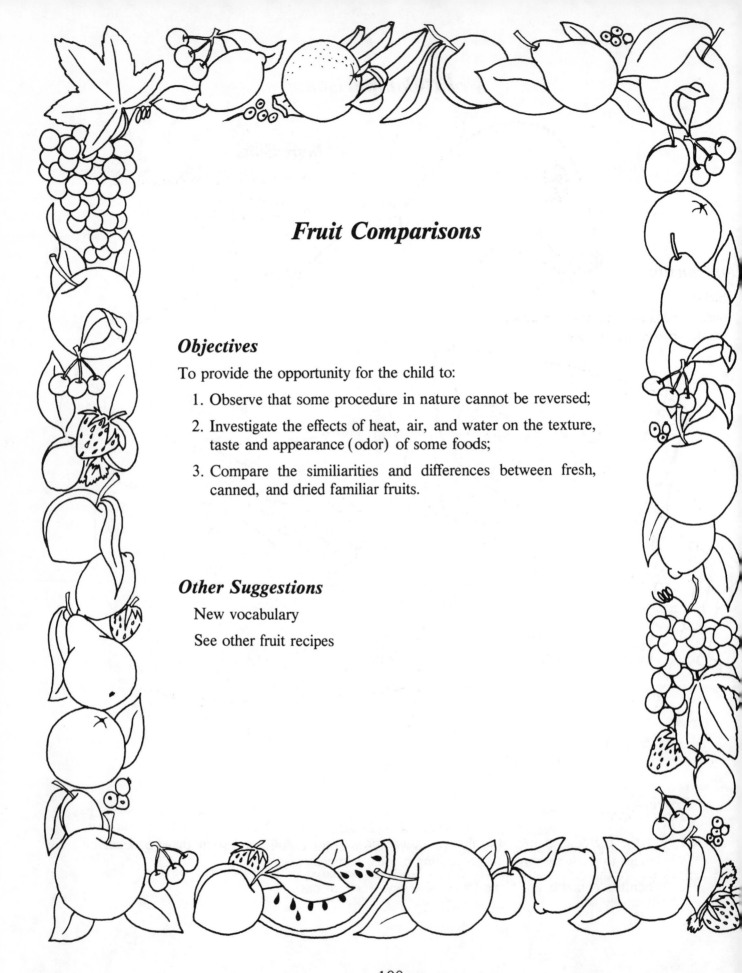

# Fruit Comparisons

## Objectives

To provide the opportunity for the child to:

1. Observe that some procedure in nature cannot be reversed;

2. Investigate the effects of heat, air, and water on the texture, taste and appearance (odor) of some foods;

3. Compare the similiarities and differences between fresh, canned, and dried familiar fruits.

## Other Suggestions

New vocabulary

See other fruit recipes

# Fruit Comparisons

**Implements**

  knives
  shallow dishes
  cups

**Ingredients**

canned, raw and dried fruits such as:

  peaches
  apricots
  prunes
  apples
  bananas
  pineapple

## Procedure

1. Place small amounts of the raw, canned and dried fruit in separate dishes. If you use peaches, for example, be sure to have some fresh, some canned and some dried peaches.

2. Compare the differences in a fruit that has been prepared in these different ways.

3. Sample the fruit.

# Cheese Biscuits

## Objectives

To provide the opportunity for the child to:

1. Experience mixing, cutting, observing and eating a familiar food in a new variation or combination;

2. Observe that foods change form when cooked, creamed, etc.

## Other Suggestions

New vocabulary: sift, grate, chopped

Blends: chop, grate, cheese, etc..

Other cheese recipes: Cheese Soup

Other biscuit recipes: Pigs in the Blanket

# Cheese Biscuits

## Ingredients

2 cups grated mild cheese
2 cups plain flour, sifted
2 teaspoons salt
2 cups chopped nuts (or less)
2 sticks margarine (or butter)

## Implements

fork
toaster oven
cheese grater
metric cups and spoons
bowls
fork and spoon
cookie sheet
waxed paper

## Procedure

1. Grate the cheese.

2. Measure the flour and salt and sift them together.

3. Cream the cheese and margarine with the mixer.

4. Add the flour and salt to the creamed mixture.

5. Knead it well on wax paper.

6. Add the nuts and knead some more.

7. Make small balls.

8. Put them on the cookie sheet and press them flat with the fork.

9. Bake at 350° until very light brown.

10. Cool and eat!

# Cheese Soup

## Objectives

To provide the opportunity for the child to:

1. Observe that heat changes some materials into different yet similar form, taste and odor while making a drastic change in appearance;

2. Observe solid familiar object melt (change form);

3. Compare a familiar food both before and after heat has changed it (heat and mixing with another familiar food.)

## Other Suggestions

New vocabulary: croutons, paprika

Nursery rhyme about cheese

# Cheese Soup

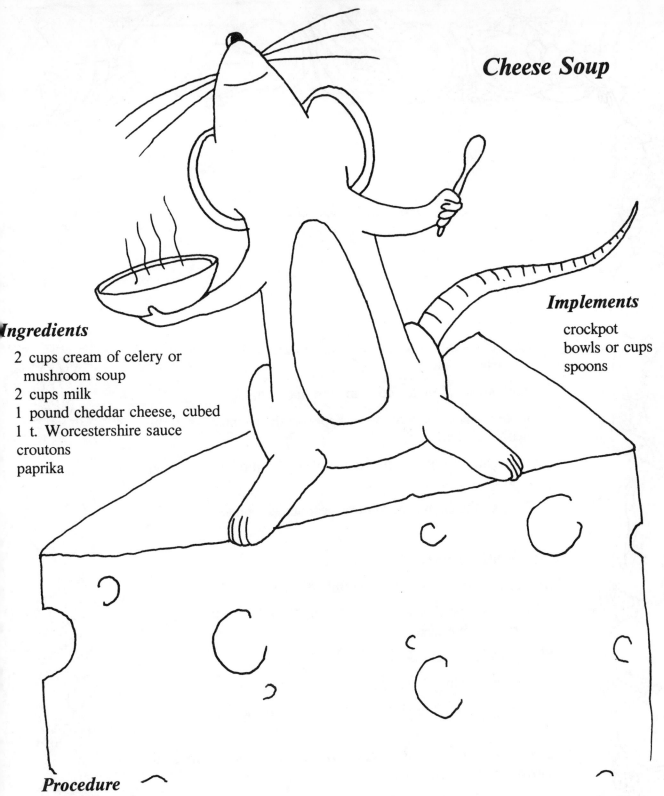

## Ingredients

2 cups cream of celery or
  mushroom soup
2 cups milk
1 pound cheddar cheese, cubed
1 t. Worcestershire sauce
croutons
paprika

## Implements

crockpot
bowls or cups
spoons

## Procedure

1. Mix the milk with the soup in the crockpot. For each can of soup, add a can full of milk.

2. Add the cheese and Worcestershire sauce to soup.

3. Cover and cook on high for 2 hours.

4. Serve the soup in bowls, and top it with crisp croutons. Sprinkle with paprika.

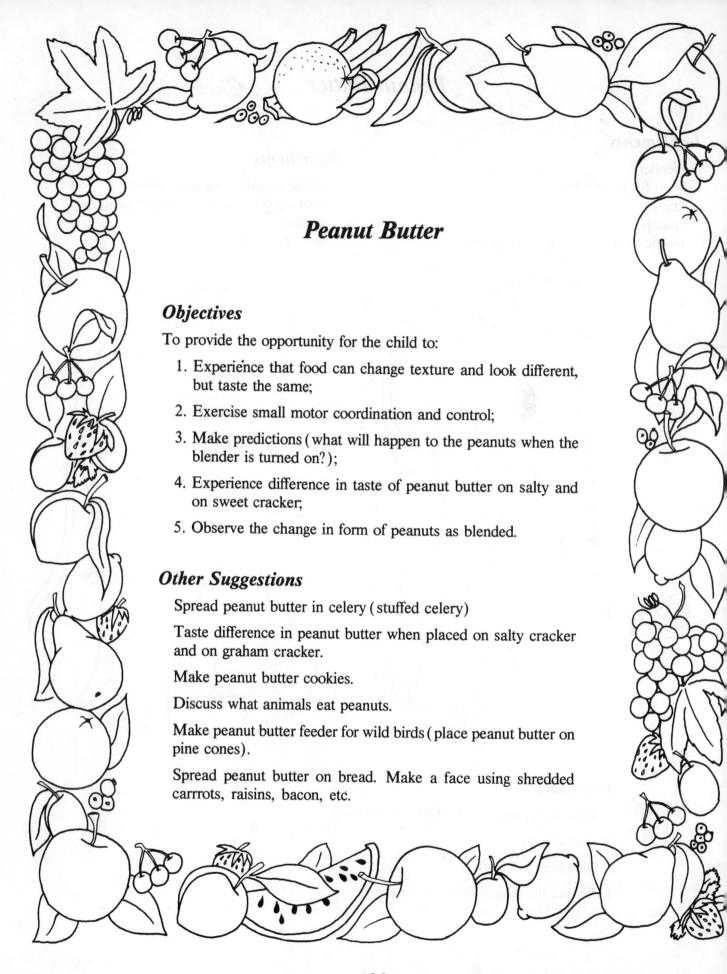

# Peanut Butter

## Objectives

To provide the opportunity for the child to:

1. Experience that food can change texture and look different, but taste the same;

2. Exercise small motor coordination and control;

3. Make predictions (what will happen to the peanuts when the blender is turned on?);

4. Experience difference in taste of peanut butter on salty and on sweet cracker;

5. Observe the change in form of peanuts as blended.

## Other Suggestions

Spread peanut butter in celery (stuffed celery)

Taste difference in peanut butter when placed on salty cracker and on graham cracker.

Make peanut butter cookies.

Discuss what animals eat peanuts.

Make peanut butter feeder for wild birds (place peanut butter on pine cones).

Spread peanut butter on bread. Make a face using shredded carrrots, raisins, bacon, etc.

# Peanut Butter

## Implements

blender
bowl for peanut butter
knives
spatula
metric measuring cups and spoons

## Ingredients

salted peanuts (not dry roasted)
cooking oil (2 t. per ½ cup of peanuts)
saltines
graham crackers

## Procedure

1. Pour the peanuts in the blender container.

2. Add the oil.

3. Blend until smooth.

4. Spread the peanut butter on crackers.

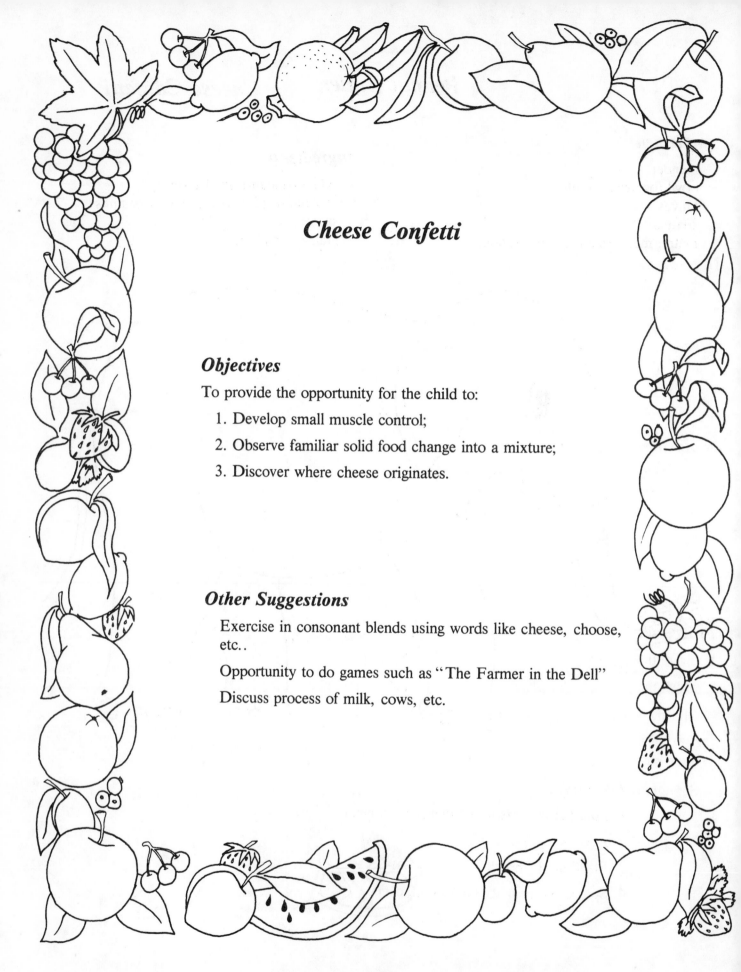

# *Cheese Confetti*

## *Objectives*

To provide the opportunity for the child to:

1. Develop small muscle control;

2. Observe familiar solid food change into a mixture;

3. Discover where cheese originates.

## *Other Suggestions*

Exercise in consonant blends using words like cheese, choose, etc..

Opportunity to do games such as "The Farmer in the Dell"

Discuss process of milk, cows, etc.

# Cheese Confetti

## Ingredients

1 lb. cheese
1 small jar pimiento
mayonnaise
bread

## Implements

bowl
spoon
fork
grater

## Procedure

1. Grate the cheese.

2. Mash the pimiento.

3. Mix the grated cheese and pimiento and add mayonnaise one tablespoon at a time until it's thick but spreadable.

4. Serve on bread.

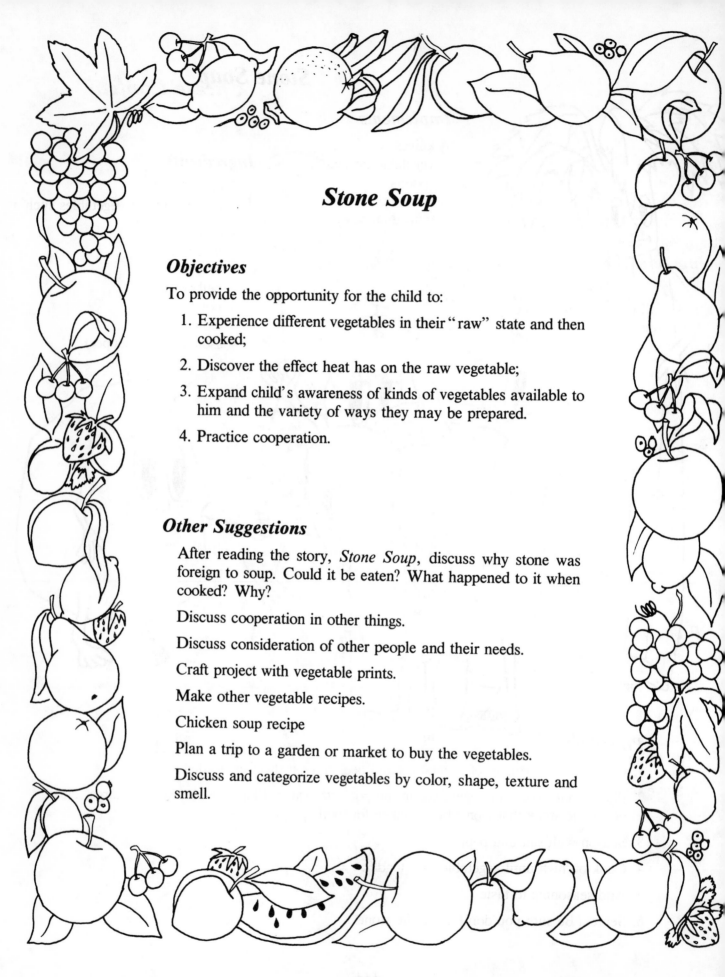

# Stone Soup

## Objectives

To provide the opportunity for the child to:

1. Experience different vegetables in their "raw" state and then cooked;

2. Discover the effect heat has on the raw vegetable;

3. Expand child's awareness of kinds of vegetables available to him and the variety of ways they may be prepared.

4. Practice cooperation.

## Other Suggestions

After reading the story, *Stone Soup*, discuss why stone was foreign to soup. Could it be eaten? What happened to it when cooked? Why?

Discuss cooperation in other things.

Discuss consideration of other people and their needs.

Craft project with vegetable prints.

Make other vegetable recipes.

Chicken soup recipe

Plan a trip to a garden or market to buy the vegetables.

Discuss and categorize vegetables by color, shape, texture and smell.

# Stone Soup

**Implements**

knives
vegetable peelers
spoons
crock pot
individual bowls

**Ingredients**

water
a wide variety of vegetables such as:

carrots
celery
onions
bell pepper
potatoes
stone
seasoning (salt, pepper)

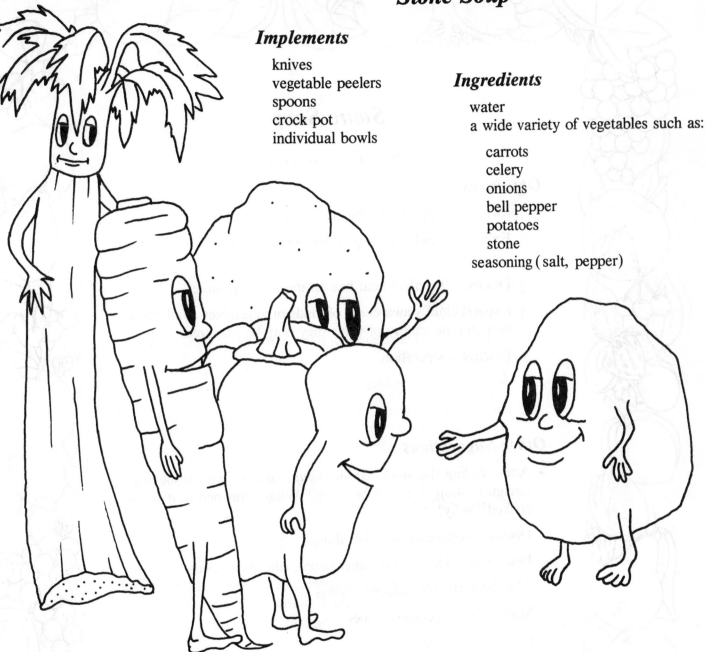

## Procedure

1. Gather an assortment of vegetables and peel and cut them as needed.

2. Place small pieces of vegetables in the pot with water. Plop in a stone (use a large, clean, non-toxic stone that won't be mistaken for food).

3. Season with salt and pepper.

4. Cook on high until vegetables are tender.

5. Add seasoning to taste.

6. Serve. (Be sure you don't serve the stone.)

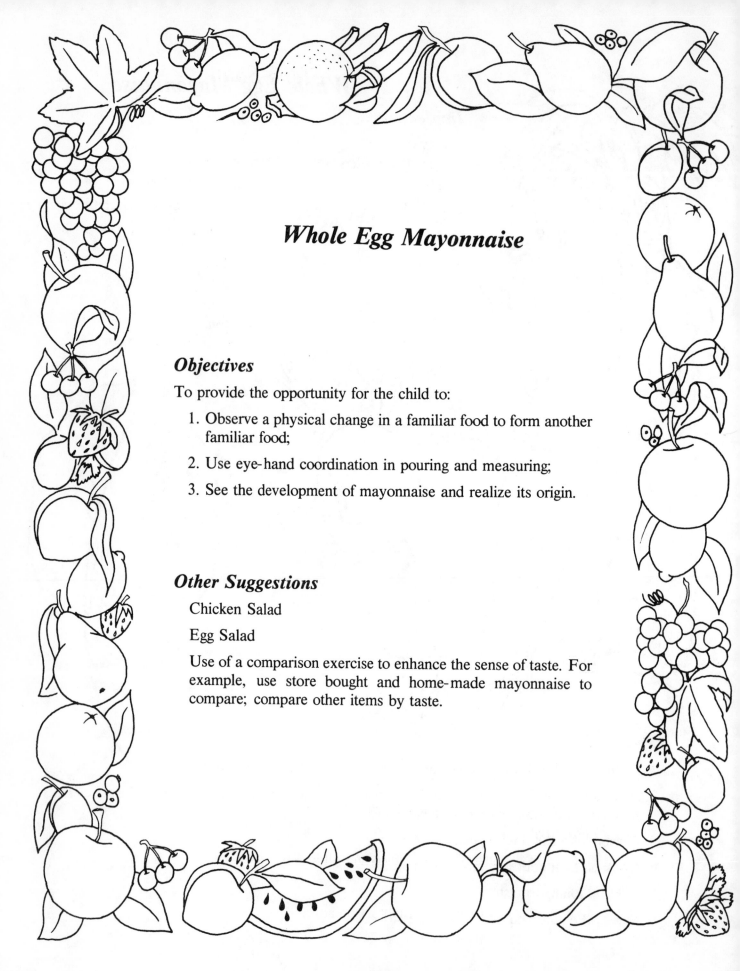

# Whole Egg Mayonnaise

## Objectives

To provide the opportunity for the child to:

1. Observe a physical change in a familiar food to form another familiar food;

2. Use eye-hand coordination in pouring and measuring;

3. See the development of mayonnaise and realize its origin.

## Other Suggestions

Chicken Salad

Egg Salad

Use of a comparison exercise to enhance the sense of taste. For example, use store bought and home-made mayonnaise to compare; compare other items by taste.

# *Whole Egg Mayonnaise*

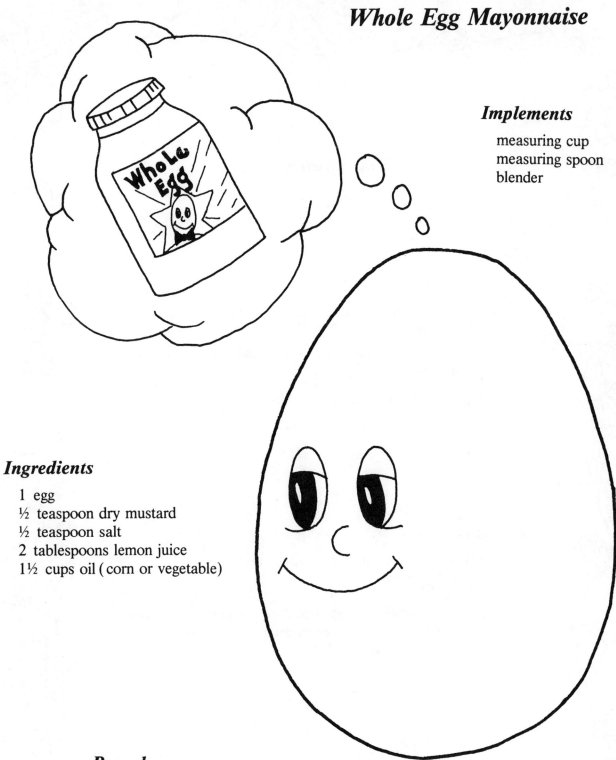

## *Implements*

measuring cup
measuring spoon
blender

## *Ingredients*

1 egg
½ teaspoon dry mustard
½ teaspoon salt
2 tablespoons lemon juice
1½ cups oil (corn or vegetable)

## *Procedure*

1. Put the egg, mustard, lemon juice and oil in a blender.

2. Mix until blended.

3. Use in various salads, sandwiches, spreads.

# Ice Cream

## Objectives

To provide the opportunity for the child to:

1. Observe the change in familiar foods which result from the absence of heat;

2. Discover that a familiar food, ice cream, is made from several other familiar foods;

3. Use large muscles in the churning.

## Other Suggestions

Add other foods (chocolate chips) to ice cream.

Milk shake recipe

Talk about their neighborhood (does the ice cream man visit there?) and what else takes place in their neighborhood?

# Ice Cream

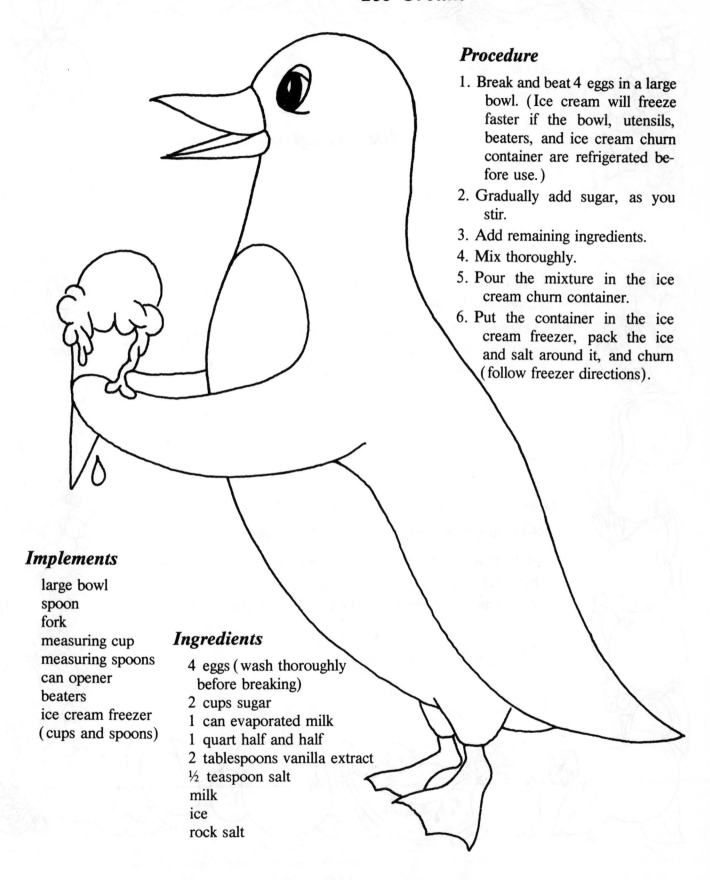

## Procedure

1. Break and beat 4 eggs in a large bowl. (Ice cream will freeze faster if the bowl, utensils, beaters, and ice cream churn container are refrigerated before use.)
2. Gradually add sugar, as you stir.
3. Add remaining ingredients.
4. Mix thoroughly.
5. Pour the mixture in the ice cream churn container.
6. Put the container in the ice cream freezer, pack the ice and salt around it, and churn (follow freezer directions).

## Implements

large bowl
spoon
fork
measuring cup
measuring spoons
can opener
beaters
ice cream freezer
(cups and spoons)

## Ingredients

4 eggs (wash thoroughly before breaking)
2 cups sugar
1 can evaporated milk
1 quart half and half
2 tablespoons vanilla extract
½ teaspoon salt
milk
ice
rock salt

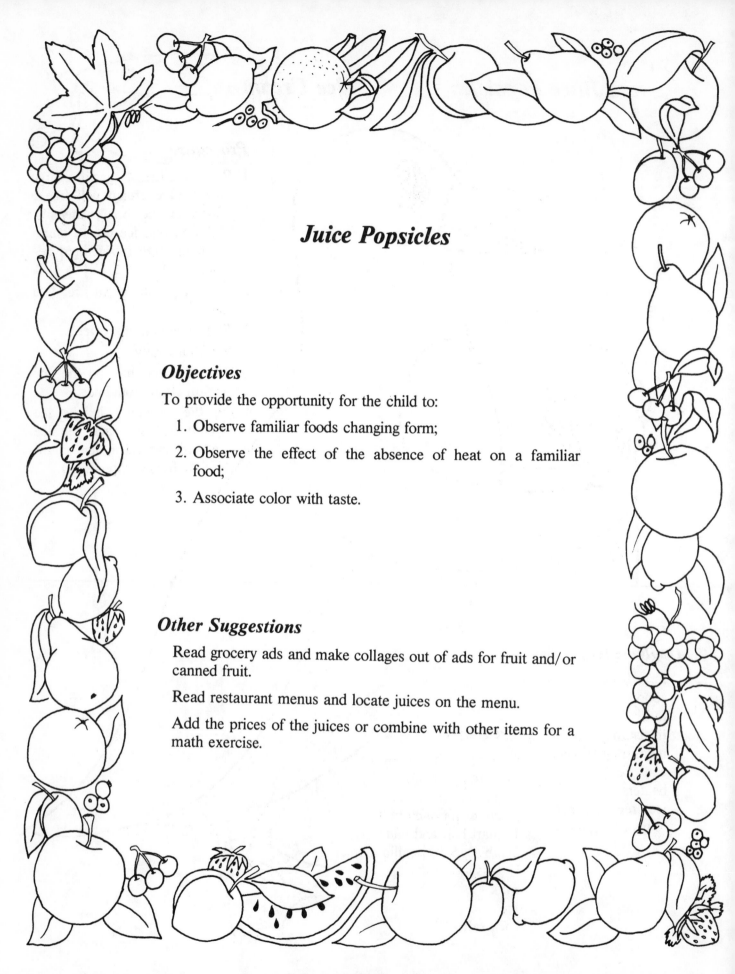

# Juice Popsicles

## Objectives

To provide the opportunity for the child to:

1. Observe familiar foods changing form;

2. Observe the effect of the absence of heat on a familiar food;

3. Associate color with taste.

## Other Suggestions

Read grocery ads and make collages out of ads for fruit and/or canned fruit.

Read restaurant menus and locate juices on the menu.

Add the prices of the juices or combine with other items for a math exercise.

# Juice Popsicles

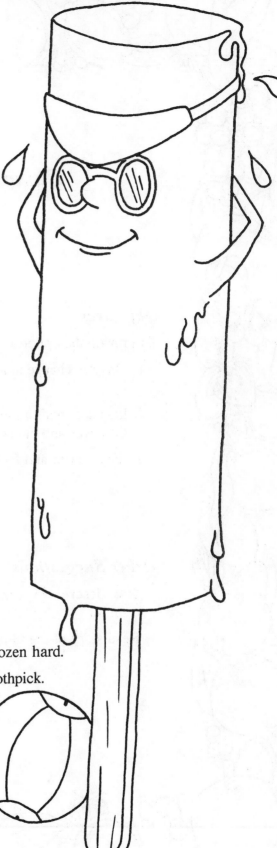

## Ingredients

cans of juice — (choose one or
combine several)
   apple, orange, grapefruit,
   lemon, grape

## Implements

ice cube trays
toothpicks

## Procedure

1. Pour juice in ice cube trays.

2. Stick a toothpick into each square.

3. Put the trays in a freezer and leave them until the juice is frozen hard.

4. Remove the popsicles from trays and eat, holding by the toothpick.

117

# Cinnamon-Sugar Toast

## Objectives

To provide the opportunity for the child to:

1. Observe change in a familiar material when heat is applied to it;

2. Exercise small muscle and eye-hand coordination in applying the sugar and cinnamon to the bread;

3. Smell, taste and feel the immediate result of the change.

## Other Suggestions

Use descriptive words, such as aroma and crisp in an exercise.

Read story of the Gingerbread Man and other related stories.

# Cinnamon-Sugar Toast

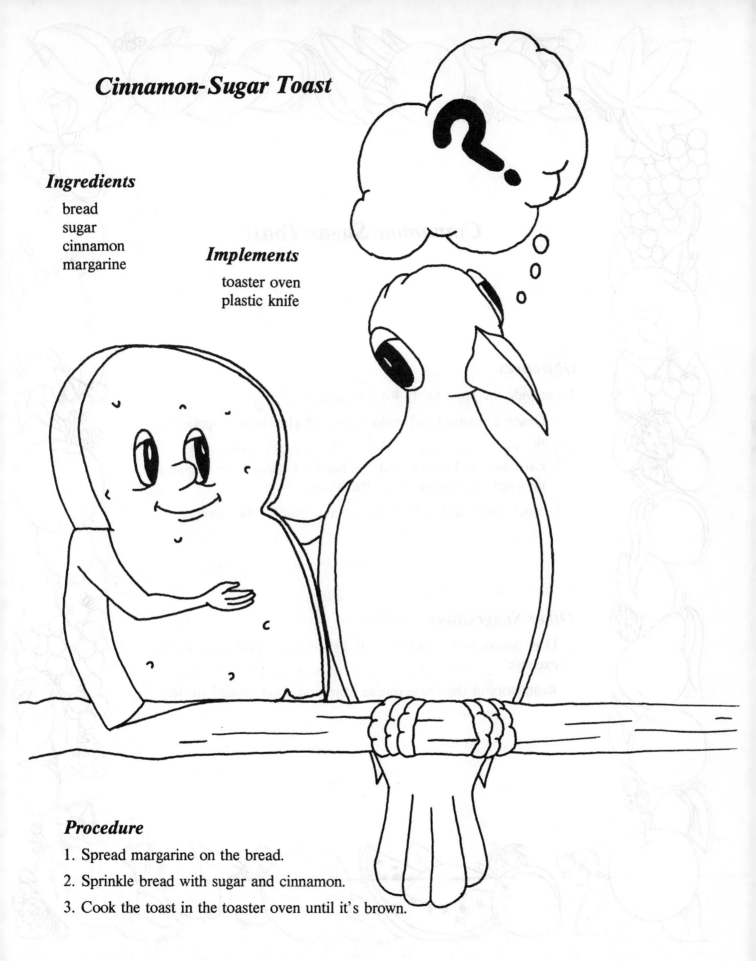

### Ingredients

bread
sugar
cinnamon
margarine

### Implements

toaster oven
plastic knife

### Procedure

1. Spread margarine on the bread.
2. Sprinkle bread with sugar and cinnamon.
3. Cook the toast in the toaster oven until it's brown.

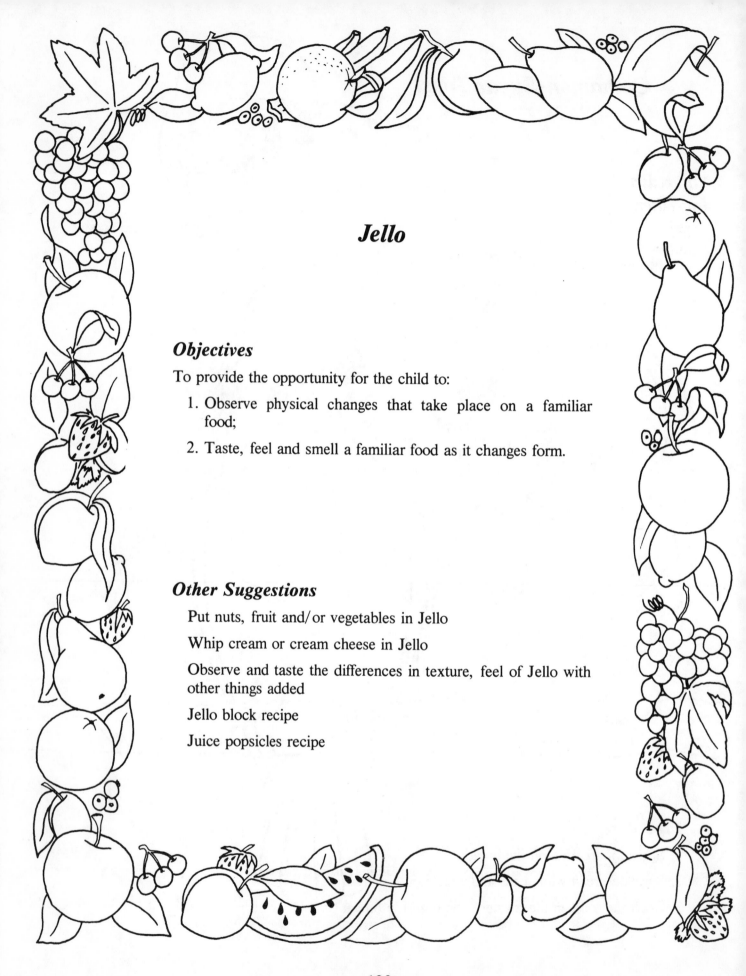

# Jello

## Objectives

To provide the opportunity for the child to:

1. Observe physical changes that take place on a familiar food;

2. Taste, feel and smell a familiar food as it changes form.

## Other Suggestions

Put nuts, fruit and/or vegetables in Jello

Whip cream or cream cheese in Jello

Observe and taste the differences in texture, feel of Jello with other things added

Jello block recipe

Juice popsicles recipe

# *Jello*

**Implements**

coffee pot
bowl or low dish
measuring cup and spoons

**Ingredients**

Jello
water

## *Procedure*

1. Heat 1 cup of water in the coffee pot.

2. Mix Jello with 1 cup hot water until Jello is dissolved.

3. Add 1 cup of cold water.

4. Pour into the bowl and set in a refrigerator until the Jello congeals.

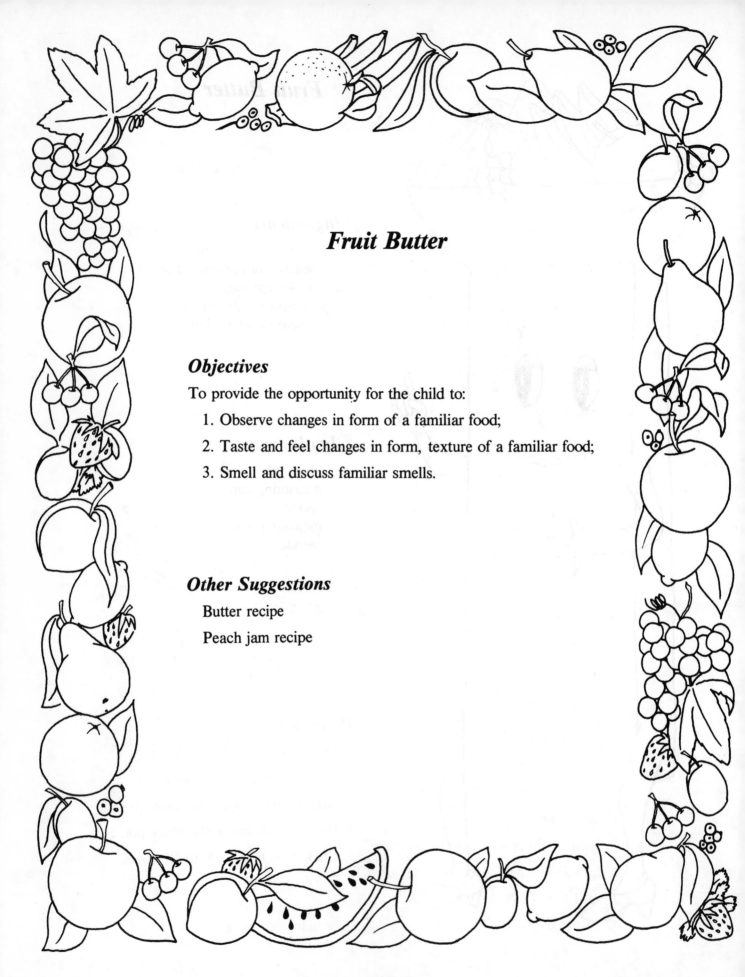

# Fruit Butter

## Objectives

To provide the opportunity for the child to:

1. Observe changes in form of a familiar food;

2. Taste and feel changes in form, texture of a familiar food;

3. Smell and discuss familiar smells.

## Other Suggestions

Butter recipe

Peach jam recipe

# Fruit Butter

## Ingredients

4 1-lb., 14 oz. cans of
   peaches or apricots, drained
3 to 4 cups sugar
2 teaspoons cinnamon
1 teaspoon ground cloves

## Implements

crock pot
measuring cup
spoon
measuring spoons
blender

## Procedure

1. Drain the fruit.

2. Puree the fruit in a blender.

3. Add the remaining ingredients.

4. Pour the mixture in the crock pot.

5. Cook it on high for 8 to 10 hours.

# *Pizza*

## *Objectives*

To provide the opportunity for the child to:

1. Use metric measurement to make a familiar food;

2. Observe, feel and taste changes in a familiar food when heat is applied to it.

3. Take a look at familiar foods that we have incorporated into our diets from other countries.

## *Other Suggestions*

Study English words derived from Spanish language

Study Mexico and cook tacos

124

# Pizza

## Ingredients

English muffins
Cheese, pepperoni, etc., if desired
One jar of spaghetti sauce
  or tomato sauce

## Implements

aluminum foil
measuring spoon
toaster oven
plastic knife

## Procedure

1. Put one tablespoon spaghetti sauce or tomato sauce on each muffin.

2. Add the cheese or pepperoni topping.

3. Broil for about 5 minutes in the toaster oven.

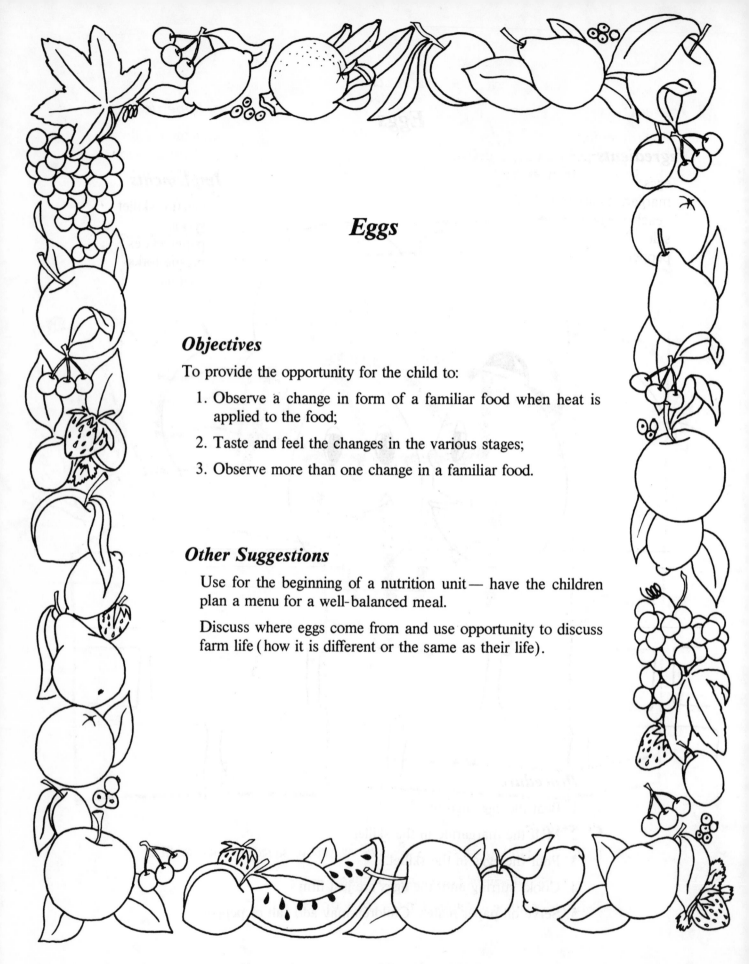

# Eggs

## Objectives

To provide the opportunity for the child to:

1. Observe a change in form of a familiar food when heat is applied to the food;

2. Taste and feel the changes in the various stages;

3. Observe more than one change in a familiar food.

## Other Suggestions

Use for the beginning of a nutrition unit— have the children plan a menu for a well-balanced meal.

Discuss where eggs come from and use opportunity to discuss farm life (how it is different or the same as their life).

# Eggs

## Ingredients

eggs
margarine (about 1 T. for
  each 5 eggs)
salt
pepper

## Implements

electric skillet
spoon
paper plates
plastic forks
spatula

## Procedure

1. Beat the eggs lightly.

2. Melt the margarine in the skillet.

3. Pour the eggs in the skillet.

4. Cook, stirring until the eggs are just firm.

5. Serve on paper plates. Children may add salt or pepper.

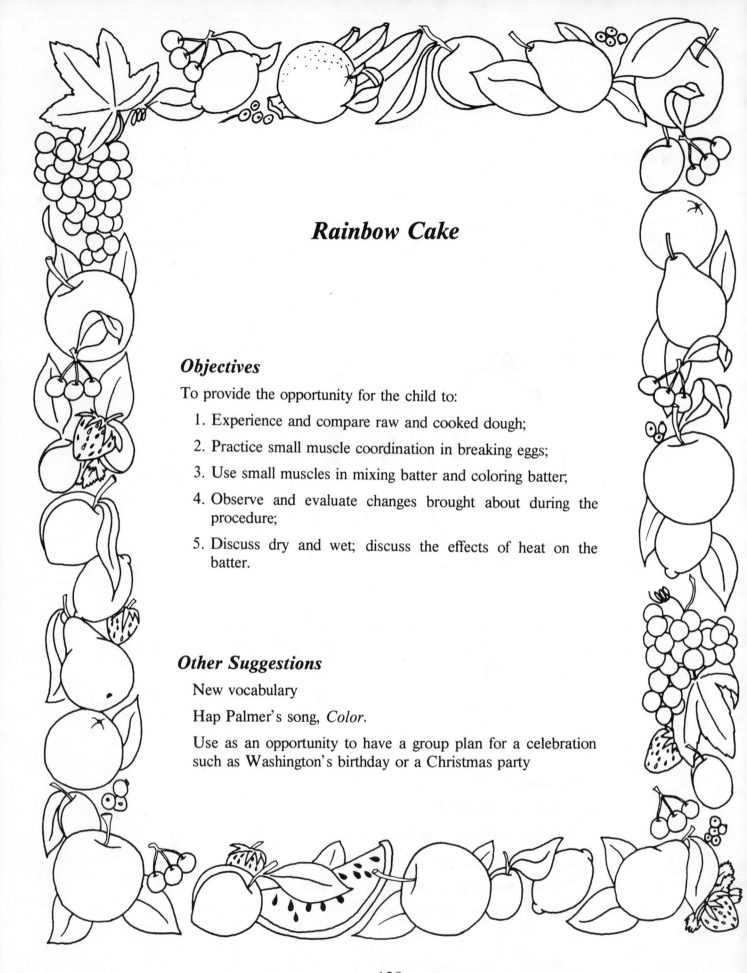

# Rainbow Cake

## Objectives

To provide the opportunity for the child to:

1. Experience and compare raw and cooked dough;

2. Practice small muscle coordination in breaking eggs;

3. Use small muscles in mixing batter and coloring batter;

4. Observe and evaluate changes brought about during the procedure;

5. Discuss dry and wet; discuss the effects of heat on the batter.

## Other Suggestions

New vocabulary

Hap Palmer's song, *Color*.

Use as an opportunity to have a group plan for a celebration such as Washington's birthday or a Christmas party

# Rainbow Cake

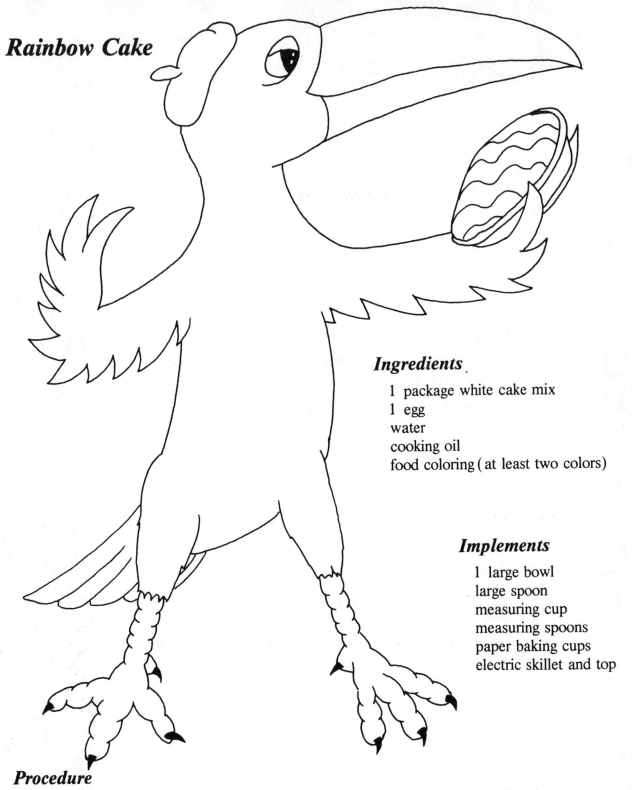

## Ingredients

1 package white cake mix
1 egg
water
cooking oil
food coloring (at least two colors)

## Implements

1 large bowl
large spoon
measuring cup
measuring spoons
paper baking cups
electric skillet and top

## Procedure

1. Prepare the cake according to the box directions, adding water, oil and egg.

2. Place a small amount of batter in each cup.

3. Squeeze a couple of drops of food coloring in each cup of batter and mix slightly.

4. Put the cups in the electric skillet and cook until done (about ten minutes). The cake is done when a toothpick inserted in the center comes out without wet batter clinging to it.

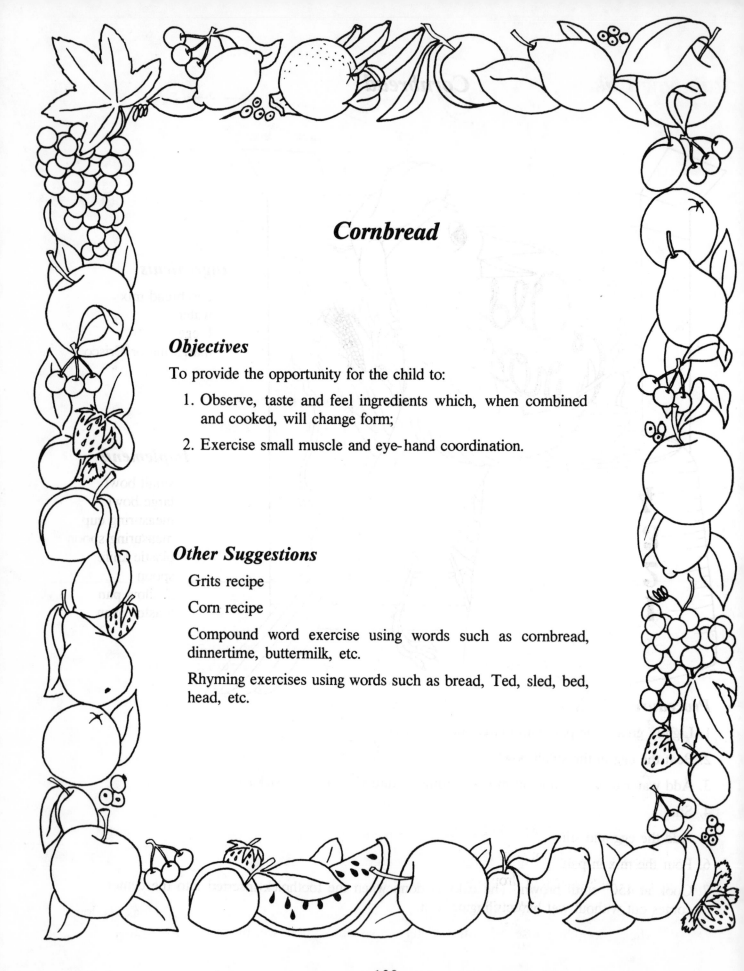

# Cornbread

## Objectives

To provide the opportunity for the child to:

1. Observe, taste and feel ingredients which, when combined and cooked, will change form;

2. Exercise small muscle and eye-hand coordination.

## Other Suggestions

Grits recipe

Corn recipe

Compound word exercise using words such as cornbread, dinnertime, buttermilk, etc.

Rhyming exercises using words such as bread, Ted, sled, bed, head, etc.

# Cornbread

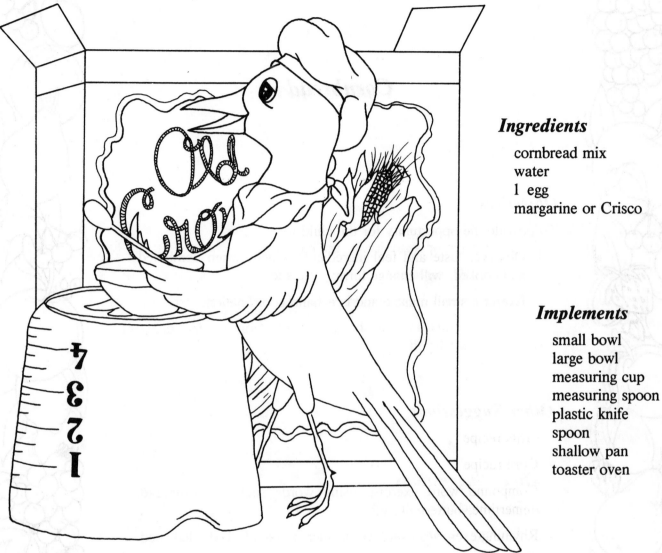

## Ingredients

cornbread mix
water
1 egg
margarine or Crisco

## Implements

small bowl
large bowl
measuring cup
measuring spoon
plastic knife
spoon
shallow pan
toaster oven

## Procedure

1. Lightly grease the pan with margarine or Crisco.

2. Beat the egg in the small bowl.

3. Add water to the cornbread mix according to directions on the package.

4. Stir.

5. Add the egg and stir.

6. Pour the mix in pan.

7. Cook at 450° until brown. The cake is done when the toothpick inserted into the center comes out without wet batter clinging to it.

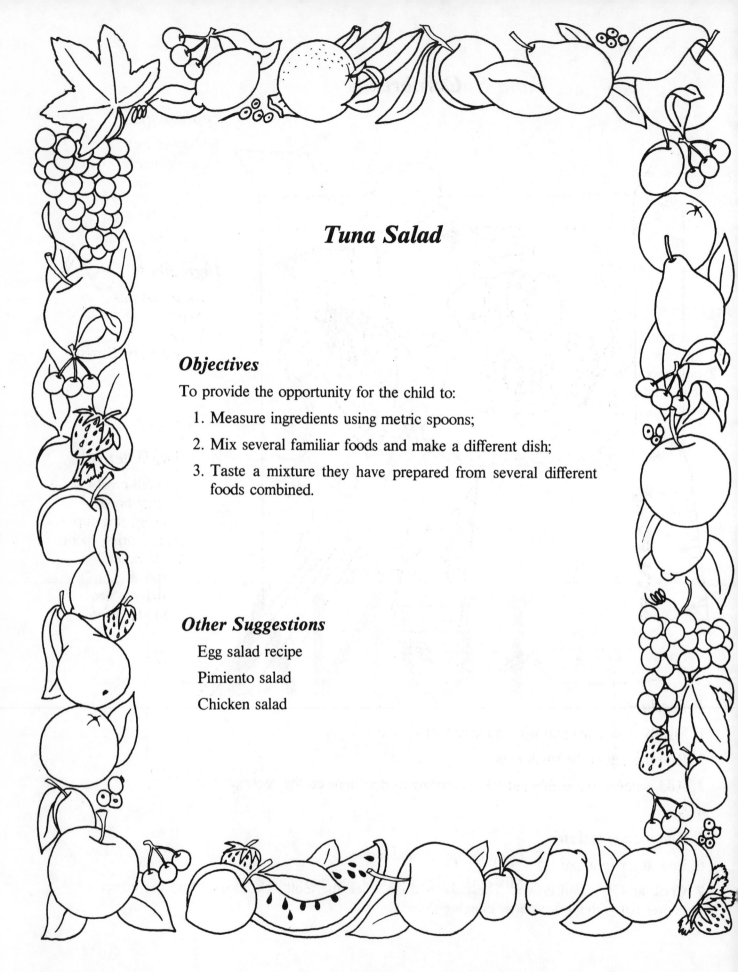

# Tuna Salad

## Objectives

To provide the opportunity for the child to:

1. Measure ingredients using metric spoons;

2. Mix several familiar foods and make a different dish;

3. Taste a mixture they have prepared from several different foods combined.

## Other Suggestions

Egg salad recipe

Pimiento salad

Chicken salad

# Tuna Salad

## Implements

1 large bowl
can opener
plastic knife
spoon
measuring cup
measuring spoons
paper plate
forks

## Ingredients

1 can tuna fish
2 tablespoons sweet pickles
2 tablespoons mayonnaise
½ cup chopped celery

## Procedure

1. Drain the tuna.

2. Chop the celery and pickles.

3. Mix tuna, celery, pickles and mayonnaise.

4. Serve on lettuce leaf.

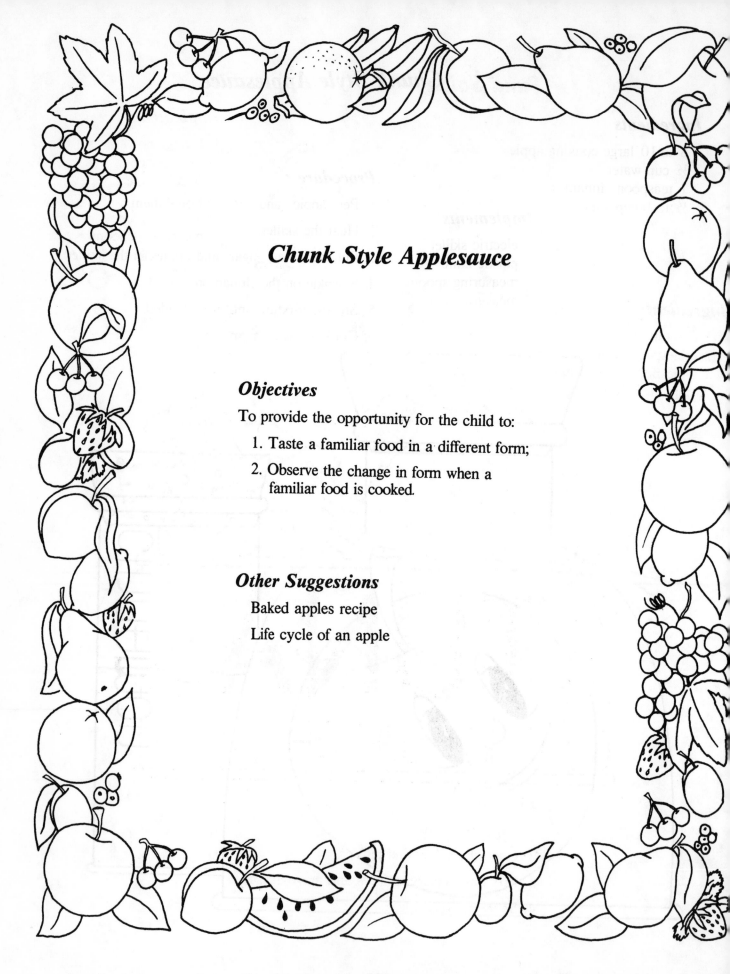

# Chunk Style Applesauce

## Objectives

To provide the opportunity for the child to:

1. Taste a familiar food in a different form;

2. Observe the change in form when a familiar food is cooked.

## Other Suggestions

Baked apples recipe

Life cycle of an apple

# Chunk Style Applesauce

## Ingredients

8 to 10 large cooking apples
½ cup water
1 teaspoon cinnamon
½ to 1 cup sugar

### Implements

electric skillet
plastic knife
measuring spoons
measuring cup

## Procedure

1. Peel apples and core and dice them.

2. Heat the skillet.

3. Put the water, sugar, and apples in the skillet.

4. Sprinkle on the cinnamon.

5. Stir the mixture until it's blended.

6. Cook it until it's smooth.

# *Appendix*

## *Annotated List of Books to Use in Early Childhood Classrooms*

Aliki, Brandenberg. *The Story of Johnny Appleseed*, Englewood Cliffs, N.J.: Prentice-Hall, 1971.

Andre, Evelyn M. *Things We Like to Do*. Nashville, Tennessee: Abingdon Press, 1968. Picture book with real photos of multiracial children. Activities for two to six year olds, including "baked cake," "stir and stir" and "blow out candles. . .on birthday cake."

Auerbach, Marjorie. *Seven Uncles Come to Dinner*. New York: Alfred A. Knopf, 1963. Story of Emile's shopping trip in Paris and how his rhyming scheme to remember great aunt's shopping list changed the menu.

Balestrino, Philip. *Hot as an Ice Cube*. New York: Thomas Y. Crowell Co., 1971. Relates the story of heat in things and correlates with Concept III. Uses beach ball, glass of lemonade and easy experiences to demonstrate that nearly everything has heat in it — even an ice cube.

Balian, Lorna. *The Sweet Touch*. Nashville, Tennessee: Abingdon Press, 1976. Whimsical story of Peggy and Oliver, the baby genie, who could change objects to candy and the problems it caused.

Barrett, Judi. *An Apple a Day*. New York: Atheneum, 1973. Simple book about apples — fanciful story about Jeremy and what happens to him as a result of his mother's idea, "An apple a day. . . ."

Buckley, Helen W. *Some Cheese for Charles*. New York: Lothrop, Lee and Shepard Co., Inc., 1963. Charles-the-Mouse likes cheese although peanut butter, bread, jam, and ham are suggested for him. Rhyming text.

Carle, Eric. *Pancakes, Pancakes!* New York: Alfred A. Knopf, 1970. Jack has to collect all ingredients for his pancakes before he can eat them for breakfast.

Carle, Eric. *The Very Hungry Caterpillar*. Cleveland, Ohio: William Collins and World Publishing Co., Inc. The caterpillar ate all kinds of fruit and sweets; then it became a beautiful butterfly. Simple story with colorful drawings.

Green, Mary McBurney. *Everybody Has a House and Everybody Eats*. New York: Young Scott Books, 1961. Simple, well-illustrated book on animals and people — what they eat.

Gunthrop, Karen. *Fish For Breakfast*. Garden City, N.Y: Doubleday and Co., 1967. Appealing story for young children about Tom and the cat and his attempt to catch breakfast.

Rothman, Joel. *A Moment in Time*. New York: Scroll Press, Inc., 1973. Story of the fall of an apple in slow motion from ripening to eating by a small boy. Only 75 words in a colorful simple text.

Sendak, Maurice. *Chicken Soup with Rice*. New York: Harper and Row, 1962. Appropriate for use with recipes for soup and stews. A book for the calendar — "each month is gay, each season nice, when eating chicken soup with rice."

Shaw, Charles G. *It Looked Like Spilt Milk*. New York: Harper and Row, 1947. Intriguing mystery until the last page. Although it's not really about food, it would be useful impetus for a dairy barn.

Sullivan, Joan. *Round Is a Pancake*. New York: Holt, Rinehart and Winston, Inc., 1963. Simple drawings, verse narrations. The concept of round is described with several foods — pancake, cherry, hamburger, etc.

# Nursery Rhymes Mentioning Food

Humpty Dumpty

Georgie Porgie

Hickety, Pickety, My Black Hen

Little Miss Muffet

Hot Cross Buns

Pat-a-Cake

Pease Porridge Hot

Little Jack Horner

Old Mother Hubbard

Simple Simon

Peter Piper

Little Tommy Tucker

Sing a Song of Sixpence

This Little Pig Went to the Market

Jack Sprat Could Eat No Fat

Peter Peter, Pumpkin Eater

These traditional nursery rhymes can be found in most nursery rhyme collections, including *Mother Goose: A collection of Nursery Rhymes,* by Brian Wildsmith, New York: Franklin Watts, Inc., 1964.

# Traditional Felt Stories Mentioning Food

## The Stone Soup

**O**nce upon a time there was a very old lady who lived in a little house near the beach. She would sit in her house and knit with her cat, Fluffy, and her dog, Snoopy, near her. She would look out of her window at the beach that was to one side of her house. One morning as she sat knitting with Fluffy and Snoopy she heard a ring at the door.

The old lady opened the door and a man stood there. He said, "Will you give me something to eat?"

The old lady said, "I would be happy to if you will be kind enough to dig some vegetables in the garden."

The man frowned and said, "I didn't ask for work, I asked for food," and he walked away.

This made the lady feel bad, because she was too old to dig many vegetables. So she sat down to knit again.

Now the man was very hungry and he made up his mind he would think of a way to get some food. He went back to the door and knocked. When the lady came to the door, he said, "Would you like to know how to make a delicious soup out of stone?"

The old lady just couldn't believe it. "That's impossible," she said, "how could anyone make soup out of a rock?"

So the man asked her to put some water in a pot and said he would go find a stone. They put the pot on and he put a clean rock in it. They waited until the water started to boil, and then the man said, "The soup is coming along fine, but if there were an onion in it, that would give it better flavor."

The old lady said, "That sounds fine. Why don't you dig one out of the garden?"

So the man hurried out to the garden and dug up an onion, and they put the onion in the pot.

Then the man said, "The soup is coming along fine, but if there were a carrot in it, that would give it a better flavor." And the old woman said, "That sounds fine! Why don't you dig one out of the garden?"

So the man hurried out to the garden and dug up a carrot and they put it in the pot.

Soon the man said, "The soup is coming along fine, but if there were a potato in it, that would give it a better flavor." And the old woman said, "That sounds fine! Why don't you dig one out of the garden?"

So the man hurried out to the garden and dug up a potato and they put it in the pot.

Then the man said, "The soup is coming along fine, but if there were a tomato, some stringbeans and turnips in it, that would give it a better flavor." And the old lady said, "That sounds fine! Why don't you get some out of the garden?"

And the man hurried out to the garden and dug up a tomato, some stringbeans and turnips and they put them in the pot.

Finally the soup was done and the man said, "I think I'll take the rock out now."

The woman was so pleased, she set the table with her nicest dishes. They both were so happy as they sat down to eat the soup, because they both got what they wanted. The man got some food and the old lady got her vegetables dug up from the garden. The lady thought, "What a mystery it is how this man can make soup from a rock!" And the man thought, "How lucky I am to get some food without working!"

From *The Handbook of Learning Activities.* Jane Caballero, Atlanta, Georgia, Humanics Limited, 1980.

## The Big, Big Turnip

*A* farmer once planted a turnip seed. And it grew, and it grew, and it grew. The farmer saw it was time to pull the turnip out of the ground. So he took hold of it and began to pull.

He pulled and he pulled and he pulled and he pulled. But the turnip wouldn't come up.

So the farmer called to his wife who was getting dinner.

Fe, fi, fo, fum, I pulled the turnip, but it wouldn't come up.

And the wife came running and she took hold of the farmer, and they pulled and they pulled and they pulled. But the turnip wouldn't come up. So the wife called to the daughter who was feeding the chickens nearby.

Fe, fi, fo fum, we pulled the turnip, but it wouldn't come up.

And the daughter came running. The daughter took hold of the wife. The wife took hold of the farmer. The farmer took hold of the turnip. And they pulled and they pulled. But the turnip wouldn't come up.

So the daughter called to the dog who was chewing a bone.

Fe, fi, fo, fum, we pulled the turnip, but it wouldn't come up.

And the dog came running. The dog took hold of the daughter. The daughter took hold of the wife. The wife took hold of the farmer. And the farmer took hold of the turnip. And they pulled and they pulled and they pulled. But the turnip wouldn't come up.

So the dog called to the cat who was chasing her tail.

Fe, fi, fo, fum, we pulled the turnip, but it wouldn't come up.

And the cat came running. The cat took hold of the dog. The dog took hold of the daughter. The daughter took hold of the wife. The wife took hold of the farmer. The farmer took hold of the turnip. And they pulled and they pulled and they pulled and they pulled. But the turnip wouldn't come up.

So the cat called the mouse who was nibbling spinach nearby.

Fe, fi, fo, fum, we pulled the turnip, but it wouldn't come up.

And the mouse came running.

"That little mouse can't help," said the dog. "He's too little."

"Phooey," squeaked the mouse. "I could pull that turnip up myself, but since you have all been pulling I'll let you help, too."

So the mouse took hold of the cat. The cat took hold of the dog. The dog took hold of the daughter. The daughter took hold of the wife. The wife took hold of the farmer. The farmer took hold of the turnip. And they pulled and they pulled and they pulled and they pulled, and UP came the turnip.

And the mouse squeaked, "I told you so!"

From *The Handbook of Learning Activities,* Jane Caballero, Atlanta, Georgia, Humanics Limited, 1980.

# Piagetian Task Administration Instrument

**Interviewer** _____  **Child** _____

**Date** _____  **Age** _____  **Sex**  **M**  **F**

**School** _____  **Grade** _____

**TO THE INTERVIEWER:** Following each task there is a box to be used for evaluating the task. If the child has performed the task in a manner that would be correct to an adult's mind, i.e., the child was able to conserve mass or a liquid, this is indicated by placing a + (plus) in the box. If the child indicates an incorrect response, place a 0 (zero) in the box. These will be tallied at the end of this interview sheet.

## EXPERIMENT 1 — *Conservation of Quantity*

Present the child with a ball of clay. Ask the child to observe it. Then roll the clay into a long cylinder. Ask, "Does the snake have less, more, or the same amount of clay as the ball?" (If the child is confused say, "Was the ball bigger, smaller, or the same size as the snake?")

**RESPONSE:**          LESS          MORE          SAME

**JUSTIFICATION:**     Ask the child, "Why do you think the snake was (bigger, smaller, or the same)?"

_____

_____

_____

                                                 TASK 1  ☐

## EXPERIMENT 2 — *Conservation of Liquid Volume*

Use two jars (a baby food jar and a tall cylinder) and enough colored water to fill the tall jar. Present the jars with the water in the short jar. Ask, "What will happen if I pour the water into the tall jar? Will I have more, less, or the same amount of water?"

**RESPONSE:**          LESS          MORE          SAME

Pour the water into the taller jar. Ask, "What happened to the amount of water? Is there less, more or the same amount?"

RESPONSE:        LESS    MORE    SAME

JUSTIFICATION:    Ask the child, "Why do you think the amount of water was (more, less, the same)?"

_____

_____

_____

TASK 2 ☐

## EXPERIMENT 3 — *Conceptualization of Water Level*

Ask the child to look at the drawing of the jar. Tell the child the jar has water in it. (Point to water). Also tell him the jar is plugged. (Point to plug). Ask, "If the jar were tipped as you see in this picture, how would the water look? (Have a picture of a container tipped at any angle). Make a line with your pencil showing how the water would look."

JUSTIFICATION:    Ask the child, "Why do you think the water will look like that?"

_____

_____

_____

TASK 3 ☐

## EXPERIMENT 4 — *Ordering Events*

Say, "For this problem, you will think about how a pencil falls. This is what I mean: (place a pencil in a vertical position and allow it to fall to a horizontal position on the desk). Here are some drawings of the pencil falling. Place them in order showing how the pencil would look as it falls."

JUSTIFICATION:    Ask the child, "Why did you place the pictures in the order you did?"

_____

_____

_____

TASK 4 ☐

### EXPERIMENT 5 — *Displacement of Volume*

Use a tall cylinder three quarters (¾) full of colored water and two metal blocks of the same size (volume) but different weights.

Tell the child to compare the weights of the two blocks. Hand him the blocks and ask, "Which is heavier?"

Say, "If I take the light weight block and lower it into the water, what will happen to the level of the water?"

**RESPONSE:**        **LESS**        **MORE**        **SAME**

Ask the child, "Place the rubber band around the cylinder at the level you think the water will move to." You may wish to aid the child by holding the cylinder or helping with the rubber band.

Gently lower the block into the water and observe. If necessary, move the rubber band to the level of the water at this point. Then remove the block.

Ask the child, "Where do you think the level of the water will be when the heavier block is lowered into the cylinder? Will the water level for the heavier block be lower, higher, or the same as the water level for the lighter block?"

**RESPONSE:**        **LESS**        **MORE**        **SAME**

**JUSTIFICATION:**     Ask the child, "Why do you think this will happen?"

Lower the heavier block into the cylinder and observe. List the child's comment about the results.

_____

_____

_____

TASK 5 ☐


### EXPERIMENT 6 — *Conservation of Length*

Use a complete and a sectioned straw. Start both straws lined up parallel. Note with the child that both straws are the same length. Ask, "Would two ants starting a hike at this end of the straws (point to one end) and walking *at the same speed* both finish the hike at this point (point to other end of straws) at the same time?" (If the child is confused, ask, "Would they both travel the same distance?")

**RESPONSE:**        **YES**        **NO**

Now move the whole straw into this position:

147

Ask the same question.

RESPONSE:          YES     NO

JUSTIFICATION:     Ask the child, "Why do you think so?"

_____

_____

_____

TASK 6-A ☐

Now move the straws in this position:

Ask the same question.

RESPONSE:          YES     NO

JUSTIFICATION:     Ask the child, "Why do you think so?"

_____

_____

_____

TASK 6-B ☐

## EXPERIMENT 7 — Conservation of Area

Present the child with two identical pieces of green construction paper. Tell him these represent fields or pastures. Place one animal on each piece of paper.

Ask the child to compare the fields noting they are the same size. Comment that since the fields are the same size each animal will have the same amount of grass to eat. Tell the child you are going to use stoppers to represent barns.

Place four barns on each field as shown. (Leave the animals on the field.)

A — Clustered Barns                    B — Barns Spread Out

Ask, "Now which animal will have the most grass to eat or will the amount of grass be the same?"

RESPONSE:          FIELD A     FIELD B     SAME

**JUSTIFICATION:**    Ask the child, "Why do you think this is true?"

_____

_____

_____

Continue adding equal numbers of barns to each field. Each time repeat the question, "Which animal will have the most grass to eat?"

**TASK 7**    ☐

*GENERAL COMMENTS:*

_____

_____

_____

_____

_____

_____

_____

_____

_____

_____

_____

_____

_____

_____

_____

_____

_____

_____

_____

_____

# Summary and Analysis of Tasks

|  | Evaluation of Task | Cognitive Level |
|---|---|---|
| **TASK 1** |  |  |
| **TASK 2** |  |  |
| **TASK 3** |  |  |
| **TASK 4** |  |  |
| **TASK 5** |  |  |
| **TASK 6-A** |  |  |
| **TASK 6-B** |  |  |
| **TASK 7** |  |  |

At which level of cognitive development would you place this child? (0 – 2 tasks performed = pre-operational; 3 – 6 = transitional; 7 – 8 = concrete-operational).

☐ Pre-operational
☐ Transitional
☐ Concrete-operational

*Additional comments or observations:*

# The Successful Teacher's Most Valuable Resource!

# ORDER FORM

**HUMANICS LIMITED**
P.O. BOX 7447/Atlanta, Georgia 30309

**FOR FAST SERVICE**
**CALL COLLECT (404) 874-2176**

| QUANTITY ORDERED | ORDER NO. | BOOK TITLE | UNIT PRICE | TOTAL PRICE |
|---|---|---|---|---|
| | | | | |
| | | | | |
| | | | | |
| | | | | |
| | | | | |
| | | | | |
| | | | | |
| | | | | |
| | | | | |
| | | | | |
| | | | | |
| | | | | |
| | | | | |
| | | | | |
| | | | | |
| | | | | |
| | | | | |
| | | | | |
| | | | | |
| | | | | |
| | | | | |

☐ Payment Enclosed

☐ Institutional Purchase Order No. _____

☐ Bill my Credit Card

WHEN USING A CREDIT CARD, PLEASE CHECK PROPER BOX AND GIVE APPROPRIATE CARD AND NUMBER INFORMATION.

MASTER CARD ☐          VISA ☐

Credit Card No. ▯▯▯▯▯▯▯▯▯▯▯▯▯▯▯▯

Master Card Interbank No. ▯▯▯▯          Exp. Date month/year ▯▯▯▯

Authorized Signature (Order must be signed) _____

PLEASE TYPE, OR PRINT CLEARLY.

| | |
|---|---|
| Subtotal | |
| Georgia residents add 5% sales tax | |
| Add shipping and handling charges | |
| **TOTAL ORDER** | |

# SHIP TO:

NAME _____

ADDRESS _____

CITY/STATE _____ ZIP _____

TELEPHONE ( )

**Shipping and Handling Charges**

| | |
|---|---|
| Up to $10.00 add | $1.60 |
| $10.01 to $20.00 add | $2.60 |
| $20.01 to $40.00 add | $3.60 |
| $40.01 to $70.00 add | $4.60 |
| $70.01 to $100.00 add | $5.60 |
| $100.01 to $125.00 add | $6.60 |
| $125.01 to $150.00 add | $7.60 |
| $150.01 to $175.00 add | $8.60 |
| $175.01 to $200.00 add | $9.60 |

Orders over $200 vary depending on method of shipment.

# Timothy Goes to School

W9-CPV-437

PUFFIN BOOKS

# TIMOTHY GOES TO SCHOOL

Story and pictures by
## Rosemary Wells

For Jennifer and Karen H.

Copyright © 1981 by Rosemary Wells
All rights reserved
Library of Congress Catalog Card Number: 80-20785
First Pied Piper Printing 1983
Printed in Hong Kong by South China Printing Co.
20  19  18  17  16
A Pied Piper Book is a registered trademark of
Dial Books for Young Readers,
a division of Penguin Books USA Inc.
® TM 1,163,686 and ® TM 1,054,312.

TIMOTHY GOES TO SCHOOL
is published in a hardcover edition by
Dial Books for Young Readers,
375 Hudson Street, New York, New York 10014.
ISBN 0-14-054715-0

Timothy's mother made him a brand-new sunsuit for the first day
of school.
"Hooray!" said Timothy.

Timothy went to school in his new sunsuit with his new book
and his new pencil.

"Good morning!" said Timothy.

"Good morning!" said the teacher.

"Timothy," said the teacher, "this is Claude.

Claude, this is Timothy. I'm sure you'll be the best of friends."

"Hello!" said Timothy.

"Nobody wears a sunsuit on the first day of school," said Claude.

During playtime Timothy hoped and hoped that
Claude would fall into a puddle.

But he didn't.

When Timothy came home, his mother asked, "How was school today?"

"Nobody wears a sunsuit on the first day of school," said Timothy.

"I will make you a beautiful new jacket," said Timothy's mother.

Timothy wore his new jacket the next day.

"Hello!" said Timothy to Claude.

"You're not supposed to wear party clothes
on the second day of school," said Claude.

All day Timothy wanted and wanted Claude to make a mistake.

But he didn't.

When Timothy went home, his mother asked, "How did it go?"

"You're not supposed to wear party clothes on the second day of school," said Timothy.

"Don't worry," said Timothy's mother. "Tomorrow you just wear something in-between like everyone else."

The next day Timothy went to school in his favorite shirt.

"Look!" said Timothy. "You are wearing the same shirt I am!"

"No," said Claude, "you are wearing the same shirt that *I* am."

During lunch Timothy wished and wished that Claude
would have to eat all alone.

But he didn't.

After school Timothy's mother could not find Timothy. "Where are you?" she called.

"I'm never going back to school," said Timothy.

"Why not?" called his mother.

"Because Claude is the smartest and the best at everything and he
   has all the friends," said Timothy.
"You'll feel better in your new football shirt," said Timothy's
   mother.

Timothy did not feel better in his new football shirt.

That morning Claude played the saxophone.

"I can't stand it anymore," said a voice next to Timothy.

It was Violet.

"You can't stand what?" Timothy asked Violet.

"Grace!" said Violet. "She sings. She dances. She counts up to a thousand and she sits next to me!"

During playtime Timothy and Violet stayed together.

Violet said, "I can't believe you've been here all along!"
"Will you come home and have cookies with me after school?"
Timothy asked.

On the way home Timothy and Violet laughed so much about
Claude and Grace that they both got the hiccups.